Reframing Economic Policy towards Sustainability

T0298560

In a globalized world economy, delivering the aspirations of sustainability is proving to be difficult. Progress is held back by competing objectives within a complex interplay of factors. Finding solutions to the 'wicked problem' of sustainability seems to be beyond the reach of policy makers. Even if the political will can be found to deal with the prime challenges of the twenty-first century, ranging from climate change and resource depletion to persistent poverty and increasing inequity, what is to be done in terms of real-world policy is far from clear.

Do we need more globalization; or has economic globalization gone too far in growing a global economy which will strip the planet bare? This book reports twin-track research which interweaves the intellectual argument over the future of the world economy intertwined with empirical research into the challenge of sustainability in aviation. Discussing the prime challenges of this century through the lens of the intractable policy stalemate in aviation, this book leads the reader to the identification of a new way forward. Whether the political will is forthcoming will continue to be subject to debate, but we now have a clear exposition of how to address the problem.

The new paradigm presented in this book opens the way to considering radical transformations to make real progress with the sustainability agenda.

Peter McManners works as a consultant and author and is a Visiting Fellow at Henley Business School, UK.

Reframing Economic Policy towards Sustainability

Explored through a case study
into aviation

Peter McManners

Routledge
Taylor & Francis Group

LONDON AND NEW YORK

First published 2017 by Routledge

2 Park Square, Milton Park, Abingdon, Oxfordshire OX14 4RN

52 Vanderbilt Avenue, New York, NY 10017

Routledge is an imprint of the Taylor & Francis Group, an informa business

First issued in paperback 2019

British Library Cataloguing in Publication Data
A catalogue record for this book is available from the British Library

Library of Congress Cataloging in Publication Data
Names: McManners, Peter J., author.
Title: Reframing economic policy towards sustainability : explored through a
case study into aviation / Peter McManners.
Description: Abingdon, Oxon ; New York, NY : Routledge, 2017. |
Includes index.
Identifiers: LCCN 2016023176| ISBN 9781138222854 (hardback) |
ISBN 9781315406701 (ebook)
Subjects: LCSH: Sustainable development--Government policy. | Economic
policy--Environmental aspects. | Environmental policy--Economic aspects. |
Aeronautics--Environmental aspects--Case studies.
Classification: LCC HC79.E5 M3925 2017 | DDC 338.9/27--dc23LC record
available at https://lccn.loc.gov/2016023176

ISBN: 978-1-138-22285-4 (hbk)
ISBN: 978-0-367-88524-3 (pbk)

Typeset in Bembo
by Saxon Graphics Ltd, Derby

Contents

Illustrations

Figures

Tables

Preface

Delivering society's economic aspirations without breaching environmental limits is likely to be the defining issue of the twenty-first century. This will require striking a balance between the economy, society and the environment using the paradigm of 'sustainability'. There is growing support for the concept and widespread acceptance that sustainability is vital to securing the future. However, taking sustainability forward into policy and practice is proving to be fiendishly difficult. If we succeed, this century could be the finest in the whole of human existence as we apply our technologies and capabilities to thrive on a finite planet. If we fail, this could be the foulest century in all of history as we degrade our environment beyond the point where we can make amends.

The scale of the task is immense, and could overwhelm our capacity to cope, but the size of the challenge should spur us on toward searching for solutions. To succeed in this undertaking, it needs to be recognized that the way we measure progress is a barrier. We use metrics such as economic growth without doing enough to factor in the environmental consequences. Allowing this to continue, without constraints, will put such pressure on ecosystems that there could be severe and long-lasting damage. It need not be so; it is within human wherewithal to deliver on the aspirations of a vibrant and sustainable future. The challenge is to work out how.

The concept of sustainability is hard to pin down precisely and resides within a number of academic silos. When policy makers attempt to apply the concept, they find themselves constrained by assumptions about what constitutes suitable policy. This is particularly true of economic policy. To fulfil the potential of sustainability, we will have to throw off the shackles of conventional thinking and be willing to change direction. The current globalized economy is like a driverless train going forward at full speed. Concerns are growing amongst some of the passengers that all might not be well, but without a clear forward view, no one can be sure what lies ahead. It would be prudent to throttle back, but when the train is rolling along, it is tempting to ignore the doubters and carry on regardless, enjoying the ride while it lasts. When I look across the landscape of society and the economy, I worry that we are rushing into a terrible disaster. I want the train to stay on the rails, and for me and my fellow passengers to be safe, but the problem is more profound than this simple analogy portrays. The situation does not simply require slowing down to stay on the rails; human society may have taken a wrong track. It may not be enough to make marginal changes to the current state of affairs. It may be that what is required is to shift to a different track.

The novel insight that emerges from this research is the need to rethink how economic theory is applied. This is potentially controversial because it requires pushing back against a conventional view of economic analysis. It can be disconcerting to acknowledge that the economic analysis on which we have relied for so long is insufficient to find solutions to the world's current challenges. It is not argued here that economic theory is wrong, just that it is inadequate to the task unless it is applied within the frame of higher-order policy objectives. This may be a radical proposal in some forums but there should be nothing controversial about bringing economic analysis back under control in close support of society and securing our long-term future on this planet.

We live in an incredibly complex world and any solutions we broker have to embrace this complexity. This is where sustainability has such power; opening the aperture of analysis provides a clearer view of the bigger picture and opens up a wealth of potential opportunities which are hidden from sight when wearing the blinkers of conventional economic analysis. Embracing sustainability is not easy and exposes the fact that there are a number of apparently insoluble challenges. These 'wicked problems' do not have solutions in a conventional sense, but rather than leave them unsolved and festering they can, and must, be addressed. As governments, corporations and other agents in the world economy learn to deal with the complexity of sustainability, they will rediscover the power of economics when it is applied as a facilitating function, not dictating policy but constrained to be in support of higher-order policy.

Within the current context of policy making, the prevailing mindset is a blockage to finding an effective balance between economic, social and environmental factors. A different mindset is needed to break the stalemate. The analytic process presented could provide the sort of breakthrough thinking required. The examination starts with a conceptual analysis at the interface between economic and environmental policy to get to the nub of the sustainability challenge. This feeds into empirical research into sustainability in aviation as one example of the intractable challenges which pepper the sustainability agenda. This combined conceptual and empirical approach moves discussion forward to a different track. The outcome is a radical view of a sustainable future for aviation which is demonstrably better. It would be interesting if other researchers, consultants and policy makers were to apply this approach to other sectors. If such analysis were to be rolled out across every aspect of society and the economy, it would inspire new thinking and could be the start of the transformation to a sustainable future for humanity.

Acknowledgements

This book is based upon research carried out at the University of Reading. I am grateful for the support provided by the University and would like to thank Emily Boyd, Steve Musson and members of the Reading Resilience Research Group.

1 Introduction and overview

Human society is charging forward, setting records for population, GDP and material consumption. By these measures, we live in the most successful era of human existence that there has ever been. However, this comes at the price of being the most destructive society this planet has ever hosted, with record levels of deforestation, habit loss and environmental degradation. There have been great civilizations in the past; ranging from the Maya in South America, to the Roman Empire stretching across Europe into Africa and Asia, and the British Empire which reached around the globe. Each has reached a pinnacle of success before collapsing. It seems that humans become so confident from success, and so sure of continued success, that they fail to take account of the uncertainty of the future and become architects of their own downfall (Scott 1998). Perhaps the nature of modern humankind is excessively ambitious, meaning people continually strive for ever more success, whatever the cost. Or perhaps people have become too indolent to look past evident success and foresee impending collapse. Our current civilization is more globalized, more connected, more interdependent than any that have gone before. If history is our guide, our current complex society will collapse eventually (Tainter 1988), and when it does, in our globalized world, it will affect us all.

These are dark thoughts and pessimistic words but they are backed up by logic. The descent of human civilization is certain if we continue on the course we have embarked upon. Optimists also have logic on their side because there is no logical reason for humanity to stay its present course. The motive behind the research reported here is a wish to tease out the parameters of a new direction for society and the economy, and to explore how to facilitate such change.

The research provides important new insights at the interface between economic and environmental policy. The desirability of balanced policy described using the term 'sustainability' is hard to dispute, but dominant policy frames are generally not orientated towards sustainability (Weaver & Jordan 2008). One novel aspect of this research is the notion that the economic case should be subordinate to the sustainability analysis. 'For each decision, the issue becomes how to make the most sustainable option economically viable. This is markedly different to seeking to make the most economic solution sustainable' (McManners 2014: 297). This insight emerged from the conceptual analysis and was tested in the real-world context of aviation. This new way of thinking delivered a candidate solution with the potential to break the current stalemate in aviation policy, demonstrating the value of the new approach. The logic of this approach is easy to defend, so as sustainability advances up the policy agenda it is likely that policy makers will start to accept it in principle, but accepting the follow-on consequences will be harder and take longer to bed in. For individual areas of policy, it can be envisaged that this new approach of giving sustainability priority may eventually be adopted. Applying this approach to broad macroeconomic policy could be seen as a step too far within the current discourse; but this perhaps is where the greatest long-term value lies.

Applying the concept of sustainability to macroeconomic policy leads to the potentially controversial observation that economic globalization is not compatible with global sustainability. It is controversial only in so much as it conflicts with a substantial body of economic argument which holds that policy in support of economic globalization is sound economic policy. Within its own frame, the argument is coherent and robust. The pure economic argument is hard to fault and to try to do so, within the current policy frame, is difficult, even when it conflicts with other factors such as moral or ethical values. For many of us, such values are important but policy makers brought up to believe that the economic case has primacy can resist the notion that there are higher order principles and objectives which can overrule the economic argument. This research shows that despite the robustness of the economic argument in favour of globalization, the problem is the frame within which the debate takes place. There is little point in framing economic policy within the narrow confines of what is considered to be 'the economy' if the long-term health of the planet is left outside the analytic frame. Leaving the global environment outside as an 'externality' (to use the language of economics) means that a huge body of academic literature and governmental policy resides on the false foundation that the global environment is not a constraint on economic policy. This limitation to the scope of economic analysis may be convenient but it means that the difficult challenges that arise from acceptance that nature and the planet are integral components of our world are not addressed. The argument made here boils down to a simple observation. It is evident that nature and the planet are vital components of our world; it should be equally evident that economic policy that ignores them is flawed. As we become aware of this, the challenge becomes the identification of the flaws and the exploration of how to fix them. This research sought to do just that.

The argument has been developed in this research that fixing the flaws in current macroeconomic policy requires that the challenge is enclosed within a new policy framework. Bringing sustainability to the fore leads to a different mindset and different priorities. The resulting framework is described here as 'proximization'. It is such a major departure from business as usual that it will be seen, at this juncture of world affairs, as speculative in nature. However, it is suggested that if the argument is accepted that sustainability is superior policy, and takes precedence over the pure economic argument, the policy framework of proximization is the natural consequence. It may appear to be radical and controversial within conventional economic discourse but as a contribution to high-level policy formulation, to suit the prime challenges of the twenty-first century, it is little more than allowing common sense to prevail.

1.1 Research foundations

At the foundations of this research is the observation that there are fault lines at the interface between environmental and macroeconomic policy, brought about by the single-minded pursuit of economic growth taking insufficient account of the global environmental consequences. If these fault lines are not resolved, society could go down a path where people will have to cope with long-lasting negative consequences such as the impact of climate change, raised sea levels, loss of biodiversity and the degradation of ecosystem services. This would be hugely challenging for future generations – and unnecessary if the current generation were to take action in a timely manner. Finding a true reconciliation between environmental and macroeconomic policy has the potential to steer society back onto a path that can secure a safe future for the peoples of the world.

In focussing on macroeconomic policy, a number of directions can be taken. This research takes as its starting point the particular policy package which supports economic globalization, as this has been a dominant theme of macroeconomic policy over recent decades. There are many interpretations of globalization, of course, which could fill this book many times over and still not be a complete review. To focus the research, a conventional account is applied of growing and deepening international connectedness in trade and investment (Hirst et al. 2009). For linguistic simplicity, 'globalization' is used throughout this book as synonymous with 'economic globalization'.

The research themes of particular relevance are 'sustainability' and 'resilience' and the context of the research is the fact that humans reside on a finite planet. This is the ultimate constraint for society so whatever else might be investigated as the basis for long-term policy, the non-negotiable factor is conformance with 'planetary limits'.

In opening the 5th World Sustainability Forum 2015, Max Bergman described sustainability as a 'Wicked Problem' (Bergman 2015). This is a term which has been applied to social policy (Rittel & Webber 1973) and described by Horn and Weber (2007: 1) as follows:

> Wicked Problems are seemingly intractable problems. They are composed of inter-related dilemmas, issues, and other problems at multiple levels: society, economy, and governance. These interconnections—systems of systems—make Wicked Problems so resilient to analysis and to resolution.

The wicked problem of sustainability does not fit neatly into one existing academic discipline. The analysis carried out in this research draws from geography, economic theory and environmental studies to consider how various perspectives influence the formulation of policy. Research in a number of sub-disciplines has relevance including 'ecological economics' and 'coevolutionary economics' (Norgaard 1988; Gowdy 1994; Polanyi 2001; Daly & Farley 2011) as well as 'sustainability economics' used to describe working at the intersection of 'ecological economics' and 'environmental and resource economics' (Söderbaum 2008; Baumgärtnera and Quaasc 2010). Clear distinctions are difficult (Remig 2015). As with much cross-discipline research, the 'great intellectual melting pot of geography' (Skole 2004) provides the umbrella for the interdisciplinary research required. David Skole comments that 'the problems of global environmental change will increasingly force more interdisciplinary and synthesis-based research' (Skole 2004: 739). There are multiple discourses on sustainability (Pezzoli 1997; Davoudi 2001) and multiple factors to consider. To wrap every aspect of human aspiration into one analysis can lead to overload and paralysis of thinking. Therefore this research is focussed at the interface between environmental and economic policy.

The opening assumption which sets the scope of this research is that the dilemmas at the interface between environmental and macroeconomic policy are at the heart of the world's current challenges and that focussing here to resolve them is likely to be the basis of pragmatic, resilient, sustainable solutions.

1.2 Research objectives

The research objective is to find a way to reconcile economic and environmental policy at the macro level. This objective is pursued through posing three research questions:

1   How could the formulation of macroeconomic policy be reframed to incorporate sustainability?
2   What specifically would be a sustainable policy framework as the envelope for macroeconomic policy?
3   How would it be possible to apply such sustainable economic policy?

Although the objective is focussed on the environment and the economy, the first question addresses sustainability because policy without a social component cannot succeed in a world where human aspirations set the context and it is people who make the decisions. In seeking to answer the first question, a key insight emerged that macroeconomic policy should be subservient to sustainability; hence the precise form of the second question. The first two questions have been addressed with a conceptual analysis. The third question was tackled through grounded empirical research attempting to apply the conceptual findings to a particular context. The aviation sector was selected because the conflict between economic and environmental concerns is most intense.

1.3 Scope

The research is directed at sustainability with a strong emphasis on the interface between economic and environmental policy. The broader aspects of sustainability have only been considered where they are directly relevant to this core interest. This restriction of scope has helped to focus the analysis but may also limit the strength of the findings, particularly with regard to acceptance and implementation where social and political issues dominate.

1.4 Structure of the book

The research interleaves a conceptual analysis at the interface between economic and environmental objectives with action research into aviation. At the foundation of these strands of research are published papers written during the course of the research. This chapter (Chapter 1) is both an introduction and includes an extensive overview of the research to present the theoretical and empirical strands in one narrative. Chapter 2 completes the context setting and sets the scope of the research, drawing on a selection of the literature and presented as an examination of the fault lines at the interface between economic globalization.

The structure of the book is shown in Figure 1.1.

The theoretical examination of problems at the interface between macroeconomic policy in support of globalization and environmental challenges starts in Chapter 3 with the paper 'Reframing economic policy towards sustainability' (McManners 2014). This chapter influences the empirical research design and provides the logical basis for the vision of macroeconomic sustainability presented in Chapter 7. Meanwhile the empirical research starts in Chapter 4 with the paper, 'The action research case study approach: a methodology for complex challenges such as sustainability in aviation' (McManners 2016a). This feeds through to insights into a future model for sustainable aviation (Chapter 5), and to lessons for integrating sustainability into policy in Chapter 6, a paper which was published in the journal *Environmental Science & Policy* (McManners 2016b). Both these empirical chapters influence the course of the theoretical analysis. The final stage of the theoretical analysis is presented in Chapter 8 and is a proposal for resilient sustainability through a new framework for macroeconomics described as 'proximization'. The theoretical and empirical research is brought together in the overall conclusions (Chapter 9).

The sections below outline the entire research process and findings within a single narrative with the supporting detail in the chapters that follow.

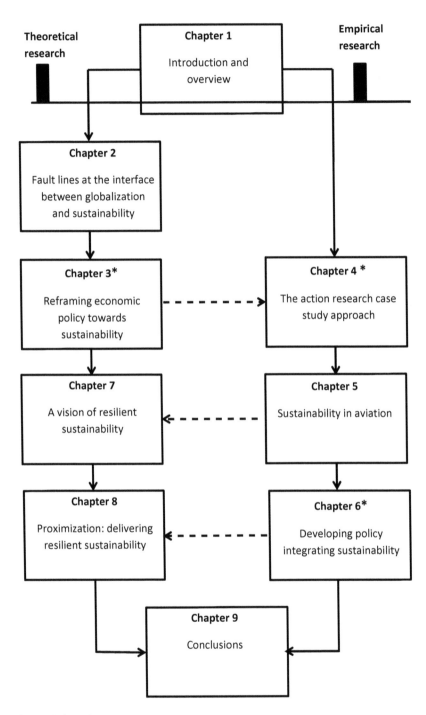

Figure 1.1 *Book structure*

Note: *published paper

1.5 The challenge

The modern environmental movement has roots in the 1970s. Books like Rachel Carson's *Silent Spring* (Carson 1962) and the Club of Rome's report *Limits to Growth* (Meadows et al. 1972) brought to people's attention the risks to society of environmental damage and ecosystem overload. From such beginnings a series of activities and programmes have been initiated, ranging from the United Nations Environment Programme (UNEP) established in 1972 to particular events such as the United Nations Conference on Environment and Development (UNCED) 1992 held in Rio de Janeiro, Brazil and referred to informally as the Earth Summit. Twenty years later in 2012, the United Nations Conference on Sustainable Development was also held in Rio de Janeiro and referred to as 'Rio+20'. Both Earth Summits debated the challenge and issued urgent calls for action. Efforts to bring environmental policy centre stage continue as the world seeks to orchestrate a response to climate change under the auspices of the United Nations Framework Convention on Climate Change (UNFCCC) established in 1992. Under the UNFCCC, the Kyoto Protocol of 1997 was brokered which required developed countries to set emission reduction targets. The negotiations have continued but progress has been slow. The most recent Conference of the Parties (COP 21) to the UNFCCC was in Paris in December 2015, at which a draft agreement was signed. The main substance of the agreement was based on what are termed Intended Nationally Determined Contributions (INDC) but the sum total of INDCs falls well short of the reductions in carbon dioxide emissions required to match the aspiration to hold 'the increase in the global average temperature to well below 2 °C' (UNFCCC 2015: 2). The launch of new initiatives continues with the first ever United Nations Environment Assembly (UNEA) which took place in Nairobi, Kenya, in June 2014. The speech-making remains ambitious and optimistic: 'In 2015, I expect nations to commit to building a sustainable, resilient and inclusive future, one that provides for the well-being of both people and the planet' (Ban Ki-moon, UNEP 2015).

Looking beyond the rhetoric, at results, nearly half a century of environmentalism has fuelled ever more discussion and delivered ever more reports but the load on the global environment continues to increase with ever greater loss of natural capital. Environmentalism has brought these problems to the world's attention but, so far, the world has failed to find solutions (Schellenberger & Nordhaus 2009).

Over the same period that environmentalism has failed to make substantive progress, the global economy, taken as a whole, has powered ahead. Capitalism has become the dominant force and policies in support of economic globalization have been adopted widely. Communist ideals have been discredited by the example of the Soviet Union increasing support for capitalism in all its forms. China has been transformed from an inward-looking agrarian nation to an industrial and economic powerhouse connected into the global economy. Free trade and market policy now rule macroeconomic policy, championed by world institutions such as the International Monetary Fund (IMF), the World Bank and the World Trade Organization (WTO). Across the world there has been convergence towards economic models with similar characteristics focussed on the objective of increasing growth. Leading up to the financial crisis of 2008, the global economy continued on a seemingly relentless upward growth trajectory. At the political level, the British Prime Minister Gordon Brown repeated the same message again and again from 1997 to 2007 that the cycle of boom and bust is over (Summers 2008). The crisis initiated a wave of commentary that the New Financial Architecture - referring to the integration of modern financial markets with the associated regime of light government regulation - may not be as robust and self-correcting as was thought (Crotty 2009; EU 2009a; HM Treasury 2009; Turner 2009). In the aftermath of the economic crisis, politicians have focussed on restarting the engine of economic growth (Canuto & Leipziger 2012) rather than considering whether the macroeconomic policy leading into the crisis may itself have been flawed.

The world faces the prospect of entering an environmental crisis whilst still dealing with the aftershocks of the recent economic crisis. These important areas of economic and environmental policy are being dealt with in different silos, so analysis as to whether the two might be linked is limited. For example, there is little coordination between the workings of the WTO and the UNEP. The WTO has the Trade and Environment Division; the UNEP has the Economics and Trade Branch; both are small operations. The former seeks to give exposure to environmental issues in trade policy; the latter seeks to include the economic angle in environmental policy. The actual level of coordination achieved between economic and environmental policy in the current system of world governance is limited (Bagwell and Staiger 2001; Brockington 2012).

Attempts to link economic models with environmental policy have been made but the results so far are disappointing. For example, the idea of putting a value to natural capital has been explored to be able to report a number for natural capital alongside reporting economic performance (Howarth & Farber 2002; Boyd & Banzhaf 2007). This has the useful purpose of drawing attention to the stock of natural capital and whether it is being conserved or run down. In conjunction with applying a positive value to the ecosystem, costs can be put against activities that have a negative environmental impact. This is the basis of current plans to deal with climate change by putting a price against carbon dioxide emissions (Lecocq 2005). There are two problems with this approach. First, what value should be shown? Second, where the economic value of an activity exceeds the notional value of associated environmental damage, there is an implication that it is a price worth paying. Such economic measures can have a useful role but on their own are not sufficient and can be dangerous by establishing a principle that environmental damage can be justified provided the price is right.

The challenge is to reconcile economic and environmental policy. Despite the efforts to harness the power of market forces to solve environmental challenges, such as climate change, the destruction of natural capital continues and carbon dioxide emissions continue to rise. Is this simply poor execution, to be solved by renewed efforts along similar lines, or could the solution be to bring economic and environmental policy inside a unified high-level framework? The ad hoc linkages that exist now have been shown by results to be insufficient. It is suggested here in this research that what is needed is a true fusion of policy. Let us attempt to bring clarity to the challenge of melding economic with environmental policy.

For environmental policy, we know what we should be doing – reducing human impact on the ecosystems of the planet – but we cannot find a feasible way to do it. For economic policy, the focus is on delivering growth – that being the target chosen – but incorporating environmental limits is proving to be problematic. Is it an environmental or economic challenge that we face? To start to answer this, let us first consider the nature of economics. We should note that economic theory is a human construct and its application is something we can control. Experimentation with economic policy is something we can tolerate, because if we get it wrong and collapse the economy the real world remains intact. Picking up the pieces of a collapsed economy includes measures such as default on loans and bankruptcy of people and organizations. The consequences in the short term can be distressing but rebuilding an economy is within the scope of human control. Now let us consider the nature of the environment. This is all around us and we ultimately depend on its services for our welfare and survival. The natural world is largely outside our direct control. That is not to say we do not impact the environment, because clearly human activities are having an impact on the global ecosystem, but human actions have consequences which are unpredictable and could be long-lasting (Crutzen 2006; Zalasiewicz et al. 2010). Experimentation with the environment carries the risk of existential damage; our actions should be designed according to the precautionary principle (Barrow 2006). Whatever else we might ask of policy it must include environmental security if humanity is to have a secure future on this planet. This brief review of the nature of both economic and environmental policy leads to proposing this statement to suit the prime challenge of our times:

> The primary aim of a combined economic and environmental policy is to reduce the long-term risk of environmental damage using the tools of economic policy to have a safe foundation from which to deliver improvements in human welfare.

It is argued here that it is not about bringing environmental policy inside economic policy or even about making environmental policy economically viable. It is about employing economic policy to deliver a secure safe environment over the long term. This is applying something we can control (economic policy) to secure a safe future for something beyond our control (the global ecosystem). This is a different mindset and likely to be opposed by both economists, with their view on growth as the primary aim, and some in the development community, who would put human welfare as the primary aim. At this juncture of human affairs both these existing mindsets are setting the world down a path of growth and increased consumption which cannot continue indefinitely. It is suggested that the statement above describes a mind-set appropriate to the current era. It is a mindset which encapsulates something we should never have forgotten, and in an ideal world would not need to be stated, that planet Earth is our home and conserving it for now and future generations should be non-negotiable and not to be traded away for short-term economic advantage. In the future, such a risk-averse approach to environmental damage may become engrained, but at this point in history the risks are so great it is proposed that the challenge is to be proactive at correcting mistaken policy.

To consider the fusion of economic and environmental policy in this way is a major departure from what has become the norm. Economic policy would look radically different if we loaded it with such expectations. Through a narrow economic lens, inefficiencies would arise where environmental requirements are brought to the fore. Using such real-world constraints to hold back the virtual world of money and markets will of course be resisted by those who live by financial manipulation and speculation. It may also be resisted by policy makers wedded to the notion that economic efficiency has primacy in policy formulation. It is suggested in this research that bringing policy closer to reality makes it feasible to find solutions which secure the future of humanity.

1.6 Research approach

The research falls under the broad umbrella of sustainability, but sustainability has come to mean so many different things depending on context and viewpoint as to be in danger of losing any real meaning. The economic perspective on sustainability can be particularly fraught with difficulty where anything can be justified if the economic benefit of a policy or project exceeds the cost of the associated damage. Reliance on pure economic analysis will lead inexorably to chipping away at natural capital to build human infrastructure with greater monetary value to end up with a balance sheet loaded with cities, factories and high-intensity agriculture. Over time we would end up being very rich in the things that attract a high monetary value but very poor with respect to the natural capital which is ultimately the basis of our continued survival on a finite planet. An analogy comes to mind of a grand house in the middle of a desert with top-of-the-range fixtures and fittings but no food on the table and a dry well. Such a building could be regarded in economic terms as a valuable asset but its ability to support a family has been traded for greater apparent wealth. This may be an accurate illustration of the world we are entering unless economics is more closely aligned with supporting long-term human needs.

The concept of sustainability has been used, and misused, in a variety of ways. The concept needs to be clarified to have real utility to go beyond the 'weak sustainability' of simply balancing environment, society and the economy, making trade-offs as required (Pearce & Atkinson 1993; Gutés 1996). 'Strong sustainability' arises from acceptance that there are environmental limits, which at world level equates to the concept of planetary limits. These are limits to which society and the economy must conform and should not be traded away (Ayres et al. 2001; Neumayer 2003). A further strengthening of the concept is the notion of 'resilient sustainability' introduced in this research. Not only should there be a balance between social, environmental and economic policy, not only should there be acceptance that there are environmental limits, but communities and countries should also have the wherewithal to respond to reverse environmental damage. This would require not only that countries balance policy, not only that environmental limits are accepted in policy formulation, but also that the macroeconomic framework should be designed to facilitate such decisions.

The prime focus of this research is on ensuring sound environmental stewardship. Economic recovery can be rapid, social upheaval can be fixed in a generation or two, but environmental damage on a global scale would be beyond the capability of humankind to repair. The argument applied here is that the priority should be the environment, but the focus of how to develop the required policy and how to deliver the required actions is all about people and society. Barriers to progress are erected by people; solutions are brokered by people; action is initiated by people; and the knowledge required to move forward is that discovered by people examining the issues. The aim of this research is to influence change in economic policy to mesh with environmental policy driven from a social science perspective. Social scientists arguing for change to economic policy are likely to be resisted by those economists who have built the current edifice of conventional economic theory. This would be a short-sighted reaction, as the social science perspective adds rich and deep insights which shift the debate from a conflict between environmental and economic policy towards types of synergistic policy investigated in this research (Diedrich et al. 2011).

1.7 Methodology

One of the challenges of sustainability analysis is that some current thinking has become atrophied around concepts and ideas which no one dares to challenge, such as the primacy in policy of economic metrics. To nourish the debate with new energy would require going beyond adding to current thinking, to challenge existing mindsets and concepts. The methodology has been designed to work around these points of resistance, allowing novel ideas to emerge, be examined and then tested.

For the particular methodology a mixed method was chosen with a conceptual analysis running alongside action research. The former could support wide-ranging analysis and exploration of ideas; the latter would be firmly rooted in the real world. Both strands of the research were informed by a review of the literature, policy documents and other reports. Where relevant, these are referred to as the analysis unfolds. The two strands of research ran in parallel (as shown in Figure 1.1, page 6). The book is necessarily presented in linear form. The conceptual analysis begins with Chapter 2, structured around the fault lines at the interface between globalization and sustainability. This leads into a well-founded theoretical analysis presented as a reframing of economic policy towards sustainability (Chapter 3). The conceptual analysis is resumed in Chapter 7 with a vision of a possible future leading into Chapter 8, which proposes a policy framework to deliver such a future. This second half of the conceptual analysis is more theoretical and less certain than the foundations laid in Chapters 2 and 3.

The empirical strand of the research is presented in Chapters 4, 5 and 6 was a much more tightly ordered process. It was designed to go deep into one particular area to explore further the insights emerging from the conceptual analysis and to test their relevance and applicability to the real-world challenges of sustainability. The aviation sector was selected because it is widely regarded as one of the most difficult areas of application of sustainability (Nijkamp 1999; Gössling & Upham 2009). Action research was chosen as the particular methodology. A variant of the methodology was developed which combined the ethos of action research with the prescriptive mechanism of case study analysis. The action research case study comprised 28 structured interviews carried out between June and December 2014. This number of interviews across five stakeholder groups seemed to provide sufficient saturation to identify the basic elements for metathemes in each group (Guest et al. 2006). The research method applied an action research orientation to inquiry (Reason & Bradbury 2000; Bradbury 2013) with a case study methodology (Yin 2014) guided by Steiner Kvale's advice on interviews (Kvale 2007).

The case study had three phases. Phase 1 used literature, policy documents and other reports to build up an accurate picture of business as usual within aviation and a vision of a low-carbon future. Phase 2 involved developing a parallel perspective from a different sector, which in this case was the car industry. This preparatory work supported the extraction of propositions to be tested (37 in total). These were placed within a nested hierarchy of primary, secondary and tertiary propositions. Phase 3 was the interview stage with five stakeholders groups: aviation industry, passengers, environmentalists, government and industry (not aviation). Passengers were further subdivided to produce a sixth stakeholder group of package-holiday passengers. The analysis of the empirical data was based on the set of propositions. These included 'alternative propositions' which equated to Robert Yin's 'plausible rival explanations' (Yin 2014: 140). These were not supported by robust evidence but were put into the same rigorous process to be tested.

The first stage of the analysis of the empirical data was to cross-reference the responses from each interviewee with the propositions generated in Phase 1 of the empirical research. These data were considered together to build a case about whether the proposition was supported, or not, and to draw out associated insights. This themed presentation of the data around the propositions became the prime way to access the data for the subsequent high-level analysis. The output from the analytic stage, and foundation for the findings, was a full set of transcribed interviews together with the same data sorted by propositions arising from the analysis carried out at the preparatory phase together with themes identified from the data which had not been captured in the propositions. These supported the extraction of the findings, presented in Chapter 5 as directly relevant to a sustainable future for aviation and discussed in Chapter 6 in which lessons are drawn from the case about the incorporation of sustainability into policy.

Further details of the particular methodology are contained in a paper published in the journal *Action Research* (McManners 2016a) which is summarized in Section 1.10 and reproduced in full in Chapter 4. The findings of the empirical research are presented in Chapters 5 and 6.

1.8 Limitations of the Study

For the conceptual strand of the research, it has been a challenge to carry out research which is not rooted in a particular subset of the academic literature. When looking across and between academic disciplines, inconsistencies appear. These anomalies are not simply a feature of academic discourse but also a feature of the real world of policy making (Pollitt 2003; Christensen & Lægreid 2007; Levin & Greenwood 2008). Confronting such anomalies and deliberately avoiding being corralled into a particular existing discourse means that this research may not have considered fully the depth of the debate within a particular sub-discipline. This is a limitation in so far as relevant insights might have been missed as the research has been selective in the literature consulted drawing from a broad swathe of existing knowledge.

For the empirical research, a practical limitation was gaining access to key stakeholders in a setting where there was time and space for a substantive dialogue. For example, a senior government stakeholder had a fixed time slot with officials present. The data gathered was useful but such focussed questioning did not allow deeper reflection and interrogation of views expressed. It was found that middle-ranking officials could offer more time and often had a stronger grasp of the detail but they might not have the big picture perspective which comes with seniority. In speaking with a middle-ranking executive in the aviation industry, a useful dialogue emerged, but when the direction of travel of the shared discussion became clear the executive became concerned and withdrew from the research. Despite the positive nature of the discussion and assurances of confidentiality, this executive felt that being associated with analysis that could be detrimental to the corporation was too great a risk. The discussion was about transformational change and the logic was heading towards a future in which some existing commercial entities may go bankrupt if the government, with public support, were to change the rules. Research ethics meant that this particular dialogue could not be incorporated into the analysis except to make the general observation that parts of the aviation industry are wary of change that could be detrimental to the viability of the current business model.

Despite these limitations, the methodology facilitated a potentially valuable contribution to the challenge of finding a true accommodation between economic and environmental policy. In the sections below, the narrative of the entire book is outlined using summaries of the chapters, highlighting key findings and showing how each part contributes to the overall research.

1.9 Fault lines at the interface between globalization and sustainability

This examination of the fault lines at the interface between globalization and sustainability (Chapter 2) provides an initial conceptualization of the underlying issues. This boiled down to two sets of assumptions and a list of issues. The first set of assumptions relates to economic globalization, which is judged to be successful, or not, on the degree to which it delivers growth, and the belief that globalization and economic growth in tandem will deliver overall a better life for the majority despite some places and some people suffering. The second set of assumptions relates to sustainability, which assumes that human society has a long-term future; that successful management of human affairs requires a balance between society, the environment and the economy; and that the overall constraint is that we live on a finite planet and are totally reliant on its ecosystem services. The dilemmas identified, with the potential to provide useful insights to help to understand the challenge, range from 'economic growth and planetary limits' to 'fossil fuel and climate change'. This clarification of the fault lines and identification of relevant key dilemmas provided the scope for the subsequent research. Without such an initial conceptualization, the research could have become mired in the complexity of the multiple perspectives on both globalization and sustainability.

1.10 Reframing economic policy towards sustainability

This paper is the foundation of the conceptual strand of the research exploring the issues at the interface between economic policy and sustainability. It was originally published in the *International Journal of Green Economics* (McManners 2014) and is here reproduced as Chapter 3.

An early version was presented at the World Economics Association (WEA) Sustainability Conference, 24 September to 21 October 2012. The starting point for the paper was that the dialogue about sustainability has failed to reduce the threat that human activities pose to the global ecosystem. It is argued in the paper that the time has come to question deep-rooted assumptions, including the role of economics. The priorities are re-examined and principles developed to be able to build a sustainable economy. It is argued that sustainability economics is subservient to society's higher objectives and is about control and balance, rather than laissez-faire free markets. The paper also took the idea further, to offer a new definition and conceptual model for sustainability that is closer to reality than the traditional models having cornerstones of 'culture', 'land', 'population' and 'energy'. It was proposed that using this model enables economic policy to be repositioned in support of the needs of society and in compliance with effective stewardship of the ecosystem to deliver a resilient economy operating within planetary limits.

The original idea at the heart of the paper, which sets the research along the path it has taken, is that the challenge is not to develop sustainability policy that conforms with macroeconomic policy, but to work out how macroeconomic policy can conform to the higher-order policy of sustainability. At first sight, from an economic-centric mind-set, this seems like a radical departure from the norm; and it is a radical departure from what is currently normal with conventional economics. If you pause, reflect and think deeply, the argument made in the paper is common sense. Of course sustainability should be overarching policy; and of course we should be prepared to change macroeconomic policy if that is required to achieve sustainable outcomes. This insight, although obvious, has been hidden from view. The whole debate about sustainability over many decades has accepted the primacy of economic policy. To this researcher, supported by the economists outside the mainstream who have reviewed the paper, this insight is fundamental to making progress. How long it takes for this insight to migrate into mainstream thinking will perhaps be a test for how long it will be before we start to see real progress with the sustainability agenda.

In summary, the paper makes the case for sustainability as overarching policy and opens a debate about changing macroeconomic policy to conform to the higher-order policy of sustainability.

1.11 The action research case study approach: a methodology for complex challenges such as sustainability in aviation

This paper describes the methodology developed for the empirical strand of the research and was published in the journal *Action Research* (McManners 2016a); it is reproduced here as Chapter 4.

Moving forward from conceptual analysis to empirical investigation had a number of challenges. First, the empirical study would take place in the real world, where the existing econometric mindset dominates, not in the new conceptual landscape put forward in Chapter 3. Whereas the conceptual study allowed unconstrained free thinking to consider a vision of future policy, the empirical research was firmly grounded in the here and now. The unusual and challenging nature of the investigation required an unconventional methodology which is described here as an 'action research case study'.

The context of the empirical research was to explore how to embed sustainability within policy. Aviation was selected because it is widely regarded as one of the most difficult areas of application of sustainability (Nijkamp 1999; Gössling & Upham 2009). A variant of action research methodology was developed which combined the ethos of action research with the prescriptive mechanism of case study analysis. This was found to be particularly appropriate for the situation encountered, where the parameters of the central problem are clearly defined and an outline solution can be identified, but how to persuade stakeholders of a way forward is uncertain. The research had three phases beginning with the preparatory phase, which examined the situation in depth to be able to propose a feasible solution. The second phase involved seeking ideas from another sector with similar characteristics. The third phase consisted of engagement with stakeholders across six stakeholder groups. The paper suggests that the 'action research case study' is particularly suited to the challenge of sustainability and may have wider utility.

In summary, the paper presents the methodology used to gather data for the action research case study into sustainability in aviation, the results of which are presented in Chapters 5 and 6.

1.12 Sustainability in aviation: how concerns about carbon emissions will reshape the industry

The first objective of the case study was to identify a way forward for sustainability in the aviation sector. This is a summary of the findings presented in Chapter 5.

In considering a sustainable future for aviation, the starting point was current policy and the current system of air transportation. The reason for this limitation was that the empirical research would be working with people familiar with current policy and the current system.

The question posed was: should aviation remain a special case for exemption from carbon dioxide emission controls or is there a way to solve the dilemma between the benefits of aviation and its environmental impact? The conclusion is that there is a way to solve the dilemma but it requires a revolution in aviation, including policy change, reconfiguration of the industry and change in the options available to passengers. The key insight which opens up the possibility of such a transformation is that flying slower can be more efficient leading to a different model for aviation where a new generation of low-carbon air vehicles operate alongside jet aircraft. The research indicated that such a model is technically feasible and acceptable to passengers although how the vision presented here would evolve in reality is uncertain. We will not make progress in bringing greater certainty to a model for sustainable aviation because it is not economically viable as long as aviation fuel remains tax-free. It is suggested that the way to break the stalemate is to promulgate this vision of better aviation to garner public support for the required changes in policy.

In summary, the chapter shows that solving the dilemma between retaining the benefits of aviation and dealing with its environmental impact is feasible, but requires massive change to the infrastructure of aviation which will only come about with changes to aviation policy. In particular, the international treaties which govern aviation need to be changed to allow (or require) the taxation of aviation fuel so that sustainable aviation becomes commercially viable.

1.13 Developing policy integrating sustainability: a case study into aviation

The second objective of the case study was to discover insights into the challenge of implementing sustainable policy which might be applicable not just in aviation, but also in other sectors and other areas of policy. These findings were published in the journal *Environmental Science & Policy* (McManners 2016b) and are here reproduced as Chapter 6.

In considering the challenge of crafting sustainable policy, the starting point was the economy and society as it is now. To have practical relevance it would have to be thus. Change in the real world might draw on a vision of the future (perhaps utopian vision) but it would have to engage with the real world. The focus was on moving beyond a transitional path to a systemic transformation based on the thinking developed in the conceptual strand of the research, where sustainability is applied as overarching policy.

The analysis supports the notion that policy should embrace sustainability but the actual incorporation of the concept into policy is proving to be difficult. To insert the word into a policy document, accompanied by some marginal changes, is enough to allow policy makers to claim that sustainability has been considered. It is noted that the application of sustainability analysis to the case of aviation is one of the areas of policy where the conflict between environmental and economic objectives is most intense. A key insight is that sustainable policy options are blocked whilst sustainability is regarded as an add-on to existing policy. The policy stalemate exists because it is neither understood nor accepted that sustainability requires systemic change. Four categories of action with the potential to break the stalemate in aviation were identified, which could also be applied to other areas of policy: long-term strategic planning; facilitation of dialogue between stakeholders; government support for innovation; and educating the public.

In summary, this final part of the empirical research demonstrates that fundamental change to the process of crafting policy is required if sustainability is to fulfil its potential to reconcile environmental and economic objectives.

1.14 A vision of resilient sustainability

The empirical research applied insights from the first part of the conceptual analysis to aviation. This was necessarily based on a view of the real world to explore possible transitions to a more sustainable future. The further stage of the conceptual analysis was to develop a pragmatic utopian vision (presented in Chapter 7). This is based on the insight that sustainability should be superior policy, and this is manifested not in a top-down global plan but acceptance that local, national and regional solutions should be allowed to develop in that order of priority. It is at the community level that the compromises required to deliver sustainable outcomes can best be brokered; and at national level where the most power resides and a sense of solidarity can be employed. Solutions are unlikely to be driven from the top down but emerge from the bottom up as countries and communities take more control of their affairs. However, it would help the process if those formulating policy at the global level such as officials in the UN, at the World Bank and the IMF were to take note of the direction of travel and interfere less in national policy debates, and shifted from pushing ideology to providing support and assistance to policy made locally to suit local culture and national circumstances. The vision is not an idealist's view that is forever beyond reach but an endpoint which it might be possible to get close to achieving, if not for everyone, at least for those communities that grasp the opportunities to live within the constraints that a secure long-term future requires.

To make a prediction now, based on observed trends and assuming the continuation of the dominance of the neoliberal agenda in world affairs, would lead through a further period of short-term advancement measured with economic metrics, to a dystopian future of the planet stripped bare. It is suggested that there are grounds for optimism that people will in the end choose the path of sustainability, but that there may be considerably more environmental damage before macroeconomic policy is put back in its proper place as the servant of humanity to facilitate a sustainable society living on a finite planet. The vision of the future presented in Chapter 7 has been crafted to illustrate a desirable destination on the road to sustainability, to provide a target to aim for in designing an alternative macroeconomic policy to enhance sustainability in a resilient manner.

1.15 Proximization: delivering resilient sustainability

Chapter 8 takes the conceptual analysis forward towards considering the particular changes required to deliver the vision. A policy framework is proposed which sits above macroeconomic policy to ensure conformance to the higher-order policy of sustainability. It is likely to be controversial because it conflicts with the neoliberal world view encapsulated in the Washington Consensus policies. It will also be contentious because it questions the rationale of the WTO.

The analysis presented in this chapter is a distillation of a wide-ranging examination of the issues at the interface between macroeconomic policy and the notion of sustainability. A number of viewpoints were considered ranging from a business and economic perspective to the environmental view and the overall needs of society. The underpinning of the analysis is the insight that whatever policy is proposed, the environmental imperative is fundamental to sustainability.

The key insight presented in this chapter is recognition that crafting appropriate macroeconomic policy should be part of any realistic solution to the world's environmental problems. Dealing effectively with the global environmental challenge requires an alternative macroeconomic framework which allows reconciliation of environmental policy with the satisfaction of people's needs. It is noted that economic globalization works if the aim is to improve short-term economic performance. Over recent decades such policy has generally delivered economic growth to the countries that have embraced open markets and free trade, but it has become necessary to question whether growth is appropriate as the prime focus of policy, when human welfare is put at risk and environmental limits are breached. Focussing on short-term economic outcomes can be a distraction and a barrier to delivering long-term sustainable solutions which balance human needs within the constraints of environmental capacity. If the aperture of analysis is opened up to the big issues of long-term human development on a planet of limited capacity, economic globalization starts to look like a dangerous experiment. The policy framework of 'proximization' is presented as a pragmatic alternative high-level framework. It can be summarized as doing the right things in the most appropriate place, controlled at a level where true balance can be achieved according to four principles:

• sustainability should be the prime basis of decision making;
• the principle of subsidiarity should be applied;
• the primacy of the state (as the most capable actor);
• the use of market economics constrained to fit local circumstances.

In summary, two important insights are presented, the first of which is potentially controversial, that policy in support of economic globalization is no longer appropriate to the challenge of the current age. Second, 'proximization' should be considered to be an appropriate alternative macro-policy framework.

1.16 Conclusion

The initial conclusion of the research is that policy in support of economic globalization, over the longer term, is incompatible with the challenge of bringing human activities within the safe limits of the planet. Such macroeconomic policy is unsustainable because no one has ever suggested that it should be sustainable; it is all about maximizing economic performance. In this light, sustainability is seen as a potential distraction from good economic policy. This research has exposed the ineffectiveness of such an approach and the need to turn thinking back on itself. It should not be about holding back progress towards sustainability to protect the current economy; it should be about driving forward with changing the economy to embrace sustainability.

Insights from the conceptual analysis were applied to the intractable sustainability challenge of aviation. This has shown that such new thinking supports finding transformational solutions to apparently insoluble problems. The current mindset is blinkered by economic barriers; the approach developed in this research encourages confronting such barriers to develop different economic models better suited to facilitating transformational solutions to the sustainability challenge.

Now that we are racing towards breaching planetary limits, our thinking has to take the intellectual step to recognize that economic models are nothing more than human constructs. Where the economic model has become disconnected from the needs of human society living on a finite planet, it should be changed. Good policy should be economically coherent but based on higher objectives than economic outcomes. A candidate for such policy is the 'proximization' framework, facilitating resilient sustainability allowing much greater local, national and regional control over human affairs. There is an element of uncertainty in proposing such a visionary policy framework but the research has demonstrated that proximization is a worthy candidate for further consideration.

The result of allowing proximization to take hold of world affairs would be a highly diverse global checkerboard of nations, countries and regions. There would still be flows of trade but these would be to satisfy real needs, with countries in control negotiating trading arrangements where there is mutual advantage. The paradigm of sustainable manufacturing and consumptions within circular economies would have a real chance of being implemented. Improved environmental stewardship would not founder on the risks to economic competetiveness. Resistance is to be expected because global economic efficiency will have been sacrificed for the greater prize of global sustainability.

In the current political climate, these are subversive proposals completely at odds with the neoliberal view of the world. The new direction proposed in this research, where economics is brought back as a facilitating function for higher policy objectives, may be bold, and in some people's eyes controversial, but on close analysis is nothing more than allowing common sense to prevail.

2 Fault lines at the interface between globalization and sustainability

> Some ecologists have defined an economist as a person who is seeking the optimal arrangement of deck chairs on the Titanic.
>
> (Daly 1977: 89)

Herman Daly articulated concern at the conflict between economic and environmental policy using the expressive language of 1970s environmentalists. Nearly 40 years later, the divergence between economics and environmentalism, far from being solved, has become more pronounced and the fault lines are showing. On the one hand, macroeconomic policy is dominated by market fundamentalism, free trade and an obsession with growth as the prime measure of success. On the other, environmentalism has embraced the concept of balance between society and the environment under the notion of sustainability, with the prime measure of success the extent to which we live within the limits of the planet. Macroeconomics has been judged a success because it has delivered growth in global GDP, but sustainability has failed by its own measure as consumption overshoots the ecological capacity of the planet by over 50 per cent (WWF 2012). It is now urgent to reconcile macroeconomic policy - something we can control - with the imperative to live within planetary limits - a fixed constraint.

The interface between research into globalization and the issues relating to sustainability is ill defined, as both research areas are umbrellas for multiple subsidiary issues. Bodies of literature can be identified within a range of subject areas from geography and environmentalism to economics and politics. From these dispersed sections of the literature there are widely divergent points of view depending on the relative priorities assigned by the researcher and the assumptions adopted. Through each separate lens, it is possible to draw different conclusions relating to the same reality. The main conflict between viewpoints is between the economist's view of globalization and the environmentalist's view of sustainability. The economist's view is heavily influenced by the widely held assumption that growth is required to maintain a healthy economy, whilst environmentalists are driven by their concern that there are limits to the extent to which society can impose on the ecosystem without causing irreversible harm. Between these simplified perspectives, the literature contains the contrasting views that economic growth can be compatible with sound environmental stewardship (OECD 2011), as well as the less common contrary view that the two are inherently incompatible (Daly 1990; Daly & Farley 2011). Benjamin Friedman, a professor of economics at Harvard University, takes the middle ground arguing that growth is necessary, not to support increased material consumption, but to 'find the energy, the wherewithal, and most importantly the human attitudes that together sustain an open, tolerant and democratic society' (Friedman 2005: 436).

This chapter is structured according to the key issues that arise, to bring sense to a complex topic without obvious natural boundaries, in a way that provides a foundation for the subsequent research. The examination begins with 'economic globalization' and 'sustainability' as they are seen when examined in isolation from each other. The investigation then moves to the key issues which make it imperative that these two areas are considered in tandem. First, there is the concept of living within planetary limits. Second, the financial crisis of 2008 initiated a useful debate about flaws in the model of economic globalization. Finally, the dilemmas and challenges identified are brought together in a concluding section which provides the basis of the further theoretical and empirical research.

2.1 Economic globalization

Globalization has a number of facets including political and cultural aspects, as well as religion, science, health, sport and education (Ritzer 2010). In the context of this research, the focus is on *economic* globalization and the terms 'economic globalization' and 'globalization' are regarded as synonymous. An important question is the extent to which globalization is a consequence of factors outside the direct control of policy makers or is the result of deliberate choice. Advances in technology which make communication easy and instantaneous can be regarded as outside policy makers' control (unless that is you take a Luddite approach to seek to control scientific progress). However, concepts such as market fundamentalism and free trade are deliberate economic policy choices: 'today's most dramatic change is in the degree to which governments have intervened to reduce obstacles to the flow of trade and investments world-wide' (Bhagwati 2004:11).

Whether such policy, to facilitate and encourage globalization, is appropriate policy is one of the issues to explore in the light of the acute global challenges that have emerged over recent decades such as financial shocks, concerns over resource depletion, and increased knowledge of environmental degradation caused by human activities.

2.1.1 Historic context

The fundamental economic theory that underpins policy in support of globalization is generally credited to Adam Smith: 'It is the maxim of every prudent master of a family, never to attempt to make at home what it will cost him more to make than to buy' (Smith 1776: IV.2.11).

David Ricardo developed the argument to provide the fundamental justification for free trade:

> Under a system of perfectly free commerce, each country naturally devotes its capital and labour to such employments as are most beneficial to each. This pursuit of individual advantage is admirably connected with the universal good of the whole. By stimulating industry, by regarding ingenuity, and by using most efficaciously the peculiar powers bestowed by nature, it distributes labour most effectively and most economically: while, by increasing the general mass of productions, it diffuses general benefit, and binds together by one common tie of interest and intercourse, the universal society of nations throughout the civilized world.
>
> (Ricardo 1817: 90)

There have been previous epochs of globalization described by authors such as Robertson (1990) and Therborn (2000) reported by Ritzer (2010), which suggest that globalization goes through cycles, indicating that the current era may not be particularly unique. Ritzer's view is that the current era of globalization has come about through a set of circumstances that make it unique and different from previous examples in history. Globalization today has been brought about by three momentous changes (Ritzer 2010: 41–43):

1   The emergence of the United States as *the* global power in the years following World War II
2   The emergence of multinational corporations (MNCs)
3   The demise of the Soviet Union and the end of the Cold War.

To consider each of these in turn, first, the dominance of the US has allowed their view of sound macroeconomic policy, based on free trade and open markets, to dominate global institutions such as the IMF and WTO. The question arises whether the notions of economic stewardship, arising from the American experience of expanding across a large continent with apparently limitless resources, is appropriate to apply across the diversity of the world's other national economies facing different circumstances. Second, MNCs have expanded and benefited from globalization and have been pushing governments to continue with a globalization agenda to the extent that the growth of the MNC and globalization are part of one narrative (McManners 2010; Ietto-Gillies 2011). Third, the fall of the "Iron Curtain" in the early 1990s brought huge chunks of the world economy, which had been relatively isolated, into a single interconnected capitalist system. In addition, the other significant change in the global economy was China joining the WTO in 2000, further expanding the reach of the global market (Rumbaugh & Blancher 2004). This current epoch of globalization is unique in scale and form, making it hard to draw relevant lessons from history.

Previous times of globalization have thrown up challenges in the wake of headline economic progress. In the eighteenth century the opening of new trade routes using the technology of the day – fast sailing ships – reconfigured the world economy and allowed the establishment of the first multi-national corporation, the East India Company. The wealth of Europe's trading nations increased but there were also underlying problems as the pursuit of profits led to what we now see as unacceptable practices, in particular the slave trade. Ronald Findlay makes the observation:

> It is only recently … that we are beginning to come to terms with the fact that slavery can be consistent with rationality and efficiency in the pursuit of profits, generating a higher real output and investible surplus than in the absence of the institution.
>
> (Findlay 1990: 4)

These problems arose from the new economic opportunity of the triangular trade between Europe, Africa and the Americas, and were not easily resolved, requiring that economic efficiency be sacrificed to higher objectives (the issue of higher-order objectives to frame economics is an important insight which will be useful in navigating a way forward from the world's current set of challenges).

There have also been periods when the world has backtracked from globalization. After World War I, flows of trade and investments declined, which many cite as the cause of the Great Crash of 1929. The protectionism of the 1934 Smoot–Hawley Tariff of the United States is seen as perpetuating the problem and laying the foundations for World War II. This period between the two world wars is seen by economists as the unravelling of many of the integration gains of 1870–1913 (Hynes et al. 2012). This period of history makes policy makers wary of reining back on globalization for fear of repeating the economic turmoil of the 1930s.

The current era of globalization since World War II is of much greater scale and extent than anything that has gone before, and in particular since 1970 with the start of the neoliberal revolution in global capitalism which became consolidated around the Washington Consensus of the mid-1990s (Harvey 2007). The associated set of problems has corresponding exceptional magnitude. Commentators discuss the arrival of a 'perfect storm' as population and consumption growth come together (Charles et al. 2010). It is my contention that this 'perfect storm' is at least in part a consequence of globalization, a view shared by William Rees (2006) and Peter Dauvergne (2010). History records that human society has found ways to make amends when previous globalizations have faltered, but the scale and extent of the current global challenges do not have a historic precedent so history is not a good guide.

2.1.2 Proponents and opponents of globalization

Support for globalization has a long heritage with policy makers in the developed Western world. The policy has benefited Western economies and underpins the advice they provide to other countries. 'The ultimate purpose of economic integration is to achieve an increase in welfare for the participating countries and possibly for the rest of the world' (Mennes 1973: 2).

The conventional view of economists is that international integration benefits all, rich and poor, and is therefore a 'benign impact phenomenon' which need not have benign intentions motivating it (Bhagwati 2004). Martin Wolf makes a strong case for globalization, from the viewpoint of an economist, in his book *Why Globalization Works* (Wolf 2004). This was hugely influential amongst policy makers to reinforce belief in globalization and push back against the doubters.

> This book ... starts from the proposition that a world integrated through the market should be highly beneficial to the vast majority of the worlds' inhabitants. The market is the most powerful institution for raising living standards ever invented: indeed there are no rivals. But markets need states, just as states need markets. In a proper marriage between the two, one has contemporary liberal democracy, incomparably the best way to manage society. Its blessings need to be spread more widely. The problem today is not that there is too *much globalization, but that* there is too little. We can do better with the right mix of more liberal markets and more co-operative global governance ... I am arguing for a better understanding by states of their long-run interest in a co-operative global economic order.
>
> (Wolf 2004: xvii)

Martin Wolf's book is a work of persuasion rather than academic analysis (as he admits in the Preface). Meanwhile Mathew Sparke reports that the presentation of ideas in this way is seen by some in the academic community as 'globaloney' (Veseth 2005; Sparke 2006). Perhaps so, but the book engaged and influenced a wide audience; Wolf argued that more effort is needed to push forward with globalization, arguing that 'in the very long run ... the trend towards globalization ... is almost certainly irreversible'. He then adds the glib remark 'The proviso is that we avoid blowing up the planet' (Wolf 2004: 96). What is particularly interesting is that I attended a lecture by Martin Wolf at the Grantham Climate Institute in November 2011, entitled 'Living Within Limits: Growth, Resources and Climate Change'. He presented a perceptive analysis using the approaching climate and resources crisis as the backdrop. He explained that globalization was a positive-sum game in which everyone benefits but, as an economist, he had no idea how the game could continue as resource limits are reached. He threw the challenge back at the audience saying that we need incredible ingenuity in politics and technology to find a solution. This exposed an interesting, and in my opinion dangerous, view that globalization is regarded as an unalterable fact, whereas, as economic historians such as Jeffry Frieden (2006) explain, globalization is a policy choice, not a fact. Over a decade after Martin Wolf's persuasive defence of globalization, the proviso that we avoid blowing up the planet is looking very apt.

The breadth of the debate is illustrated by the contrary view, that globalization is flawed. This perspective crosses the political divide, with critics from the political left using terms such as 'neoliberalism' and the 'New Imperialism' (Harvey 2007), drawing on anti-capitalism and resistance to the role of corporations, while the anti-globalist political right focusses on national identity, sovereignty and self-reliance, which extend easily to a fortress mentality on immigration (Bhagwati 2004). The anti-globalization movement is highly diverse and tends to complain at the negative consequences and perceived injustices rather than offer any coherent policy alternative. Conflicting and contradictory viewpoints grouped together under 'anti-globalization' do not form a convincing coordinated case against globalization, but it is my view that this is because of a lack of a coherent alternative. There are substantive concerns, which are jumbled and confused, that point to the need to question globalization with a view to finding a better policy framework.

At the global level, an important axis of disagreement is the North–South divide. The International Forum on Globalization (IFG) is a leading critic of globalization from this perspective. Board member Vandana Shiva, an Indian activist working to save the Himalayan forests and leading campaigner to protect Indian farmers, writes: 'The WTO rules violate principles of human rights and ecological survival. They violate rules of justice and sustainability. They are rules of warfare against the people and the planet' (Shiva 2006: 124).

A prominent critic of globalization is Joseph Stiglitz, the American economist who served as Chief Economist at the World Bank 1997–2000 and is now professor at Columbia University. In *Globalization and its Discontents* (Stiglitz 2002), he states 'Globalization today is not working for many of the world's poor. It is not working for much of the environment. It is not working for stability of the global economy' (Stiglitz 2002: 214). He points towards weak global governance; particularly in world economic institutions such as the IMF, WTO and World Bank, which are dominated by a parochial world view advocated by the United States. He went on to propose a solution in *Making Globalization Work* arguing that 'We can restructure globalization so that those in both the developed and the developing world, the current and future generations, can all benefit' (Stiglitz 2006: 24). The problem, from Stiglitz's perspective, is 'unfortunately, economic globalization has outpaced political globalization' (Stiglitz 2008: 309). I find Stiglitz's criticism to be useful and insightful but there is weakness in his argument that globalization can be reinforced and made to work. He points to this weakness in his own words:

Making *globalization* work will be of little use if we cannot solve our global environmental problems. Our atmosphere and oceans are global resources; *globalization* and so-called economic progress have enhanced our ability to exploit these resources more ruthlessly and at a pace faster than our ability to manage them has grown.

(Stiglitz 2006: 184)

The literature contains many complaints about globalization but the statement above defines very precisely the coherent argument against globalization. I have to declare a personal interest, as I am a strong advocate for changing globalization but I do not want to be classified as an anti-globalist for fear of association with muddled thinking. My complaint is simple: globalization is preventing the solution of our environmental problems; if opposition focussed on this one issue, I believe that this could become a credible unified global movement to counter economic globalization.

2.1.3 The rationale for globalization

Drawing on persistent themes which permeate the literature, the essence of the rationale for globalization can be broken down into three straightforward assumptions.

Assumption 1: Policy in support of globalization is driven by economic theory

Having defined the term 'globalization' in this research as being synonymous with 'economic globalization', this seems like a pedestrian statement of the obvious. There are multiple other dimensions of globalization when taken in a broader context, of course, but it is important to recognize the dominant role of economic theory. There is a fundamental question which is hidden if the assumption that we are relying on economic theory is not stated explicitly. The question is whether economic theory should be allowed to drive international policy. It is natural for an economist to argue, yes, of course economic theory should drive international policy, but I intend to show through this research that the tendency to give prominence to the economic view is a part of the problem making it hard to find resilient sustainable solutions.

Assumption 2: Economic policy is judged to be successful, or not, on the degree to which it delivers growth

Conventional economic policy focusses on the paradigm of ever-expanding growth. This has become firmly entrenched in government policy across the developed countries, and countries in the developing world heeding advice from the IMF and the World Bank. This is current policy to suit the short to medium term with little analysis given to the long-term possibilities of continued growth and what the associated consequences might be. The assumption that growth is necessary and desirable is deeply rooted and seldom questioned in the mainstream literature. Economic textbooks discuss what it takes to achieve and maintain growth (Jones 2002) without providing a deeper justification than a desire for economic progress, to earn more than the year before, to own more than in the past, to consume more each year. This equates material consumption with human progress, thus establishing a progression that mathematically must have a finite end. An early critic of the logic of continual growth was the economist John Mill, who argued that 'increase of wealth is not boundless' in his chapter 'Of the Stationary State' in *Principles of Political Economy* (Mill [1848] 1909). It can be argued that he was wrong to be concerned, as growth has indeed continued but, as was noted earlier, the world is facing, for the first time in human history, the prospect of human demands exceeding the capacity of the planet.

Much of the recent economics literature is not strong on the issue of 'limits to growth' – perhaps because it brings into question the foundations of mainstream economics – so this will be covered under the section on sustainability later in this chapter, where there is more extensive analysis.

The dominance of the growth paradigm, over not just economic policy but policy in general, is illustrated by this extract from research aimed at improving global governance from the John F. Kennedy School of Government, Harvard University:

> while development is a broad concept entailing the raising of human capabilities in general, we believe increasing economic growth rates is the central challenge that developing nations face. Higher levels of living standards are the most direct route to achieving improvements in social and human indicators. Reform strategies should be principally targeted at raising rates of growth – that is, they should be growth strategies.
>
> (Hausmann et al. 2008: 324)

Assumption 3: Globalization and economic growth in tandem will deliver overall a better life for the majority despite some places and some people suffering

The notion that shared prosperity increases with overall growth in the economy is captured in the phrase attributed to John F. Kennedy, 'a rising tide lifts all boats'. This idea conveys the notion that any action that grows the economy is intrinsically good. When the concept is applied at international level, the argument goes that growing the global economy is inherently beneficial to humanity as a whole, a view championed by neoliberals in the United States: 'This vision of shared prosperity is not only demanded by the global, interdependent economy, but rooted in the historic values of the progressive vision of the United States' (Sperling 2007: n.p.).

It is arithmetically correct that economic growth which raises overall GDP increases average GDP per head. However, this tautology hides the fact that not everyone is a beneficiary. Not every person in a country benefits from an increase in GDP and not every country benefits from rising global GDP. This applies even to developed countries (which have been most vocal in supporting the growth paradigm) when growth in their own economies starts to falter:

> for the last two decades the tide has no longer been rising for most people in the US, and since 1990, give or take a year or so, it has stopped rising in Europe and Japan too. So, a change of direction need not be very painful to those who have been flattened, rather than floated, by the economic development juggernaut.
>
> (Ayres 1998: xiv)

This viewpoint from Robert Ayres is particularly interesting because he is an ardent economic optimist who argued against the pessimism of *Limits to Growth* (Meadows et al. 1972), but by 1998 was starting to change his view, and by 2006 had accepted that exponential growth can no longer be taken for granted.

> Perpetual economic growth is an extrapolation from history and a pious hope for the future, not a law of nature. There are a number of drivers of past growth in the industrialized countries that are now showing signs of saturation or exhaustion.
>
> (Ayres 2006: 1190)

Robert Ayres teams up with sustainability analyst and strategist Benjamin Warr to state the current presumption of perpetual and inevitable economic growth, and to question it:

> Governments, businesses and institutions are now, and have been for several decades, effectively addicted to the presumption of perpetual and inevitable economic growth. Any suggestion that growth might not continue indefinitely (or that it might not be a good thing) is ignored and derided ... We think, on the contrary, that the emperor probably has no clothes. In short, future GDP growth is not only not guaranteed, it is more than likely to end within a few decades.
>
> (Ayres & Warr 2010: 309)

Unquestioning acceptance of these three assumptions acts as blinkers for policy makers to avoid adjusting economic policy to deal with negative consequences. This research questions all three assumptions and thereby questions the foundations of globalization, to consider whether this continues to be a sound basis for international policy or whether changes are required and, if so, what they might be.

2.1.4 The Washington Consensus

There is not one definitive policy package which can be identified as *the* policy of globalization. However, the Washington Consensus policy package captures the essence in a set of views about effective economic development strategies associated with Washington-based institutions: the IMF, the World Bank, and the US Treasury (Serra et al. 2008). This policy package is widely credited as helping to drive globalization since the economist John Williamson coined the term in 1989. Williamson described a set of ten economic policy prescriptions that he considered constituted the 'standard' reform package promoted for developing countries by the IMF and World Bank. The prescriptions encompassed policies such as opening with respect to both international trade and investment, and the expansion of market forces within the economy. The Asian crisis of 1997 exposed shortcomings (IMF 2000), but it would be another decade before the inadequacies of the Washington Consensus became the subject of a substantive debate in the mainstream literature.

In a chapter in a book published in 2008, looking back at the impact of the consensus in the years since 1989, John Williamson reflected that a better name might have been 'universal convergence' since the extent of the agreement runs far wider than Washington (Williamson 2008). He concludes that despite opposition to the Washington Consensus over the years, the only issue where he was uncomfortable was that equity did not play a larger role:

> When a serious economist attacks the Washington Consensus, the world at large may interpret that as saying that they believe there is a serious intellectual case against disciplined macroeconomic policies, the use of markets, and trade liberalization.
>
> (Williamson 2008: 30)

Other researchers are more critical, arguing that the policy reforms of the Washington Consensus are flawed ideology. This comment from over a decade ago describes a viewpoint that has gathered support over the intervening years (Rodrik 2006; Cowling & Tomlinson 2011):

> Something is clearly wrong. Maintaining that globalization as we know it is the way to go and that, if the Washington consensus policies have not borne fruit so far, they will surely do so in the future, is to replace empiricism with ideology.
>
> (Milanovic 2003: 679)

A view is slowly emerging that the Washington Consensus should no longer be the basis of macroeconomic policy. Dani Rodrik wrote prophetically in 2006, 'The debate now is not over whether the Washington Consensus is dead or alive, but over what will replace it' (Rodrik 2006: 974). More recently, Cowling and Tomlinson (2011) explain growing dissatisfaction with the neoliberal economic paradigm that has dominated economic policy over the last 30 years and propose that the twenty-first century needs a new approach to economic management. What that new approach might comprise is one of the challenges in economics today.

2.2 Sustainability

Sustainability can be summarized as the concept of finding balance between the economy, society and the environment, to ensure sound stewardship of the ecosystem and responsible use of resources. The lineage of sustainability is generally credited to the World Commission on Environment and Development (WCED) (1983–1987) chaired by Gro Harlem Brundtland. The WCED defined sustainable development as: 'development that meets the needs of the present without compromising the ability of future generations to meet their own needs' (WCED 1987: 1).

David Demeritt (2011: 240) has tracked the history of the idea of sustainable development from a narrow concern with maximizing the yield of economic resources to become broader and more multi-dimensional but he warns: 'It might be charged that the notion of sustainable development is little more than a fudge that skirts over all of the difficult political and economic conflicts entailed by those questions about sustaining what, how, and for whom.'

There is a growing body of literature on sustainability to the extent that 'sustainability science' is becoming a subject in its own right (Kates 2010). In this section the rationale for sustainability is explored, as it applies to the aims of this research, to ensure that we start on a path towards useful policy and avoid David Demeritt's concern that sustainable development may be little more than a fudge. First, let us consider the central issue, when discussing economic goals alongside environmental objectives, of whether there are limits to growth.

2.2.1 Limits to growth

The warning that the global economy is on a dangerous trajectory was made in 1972 in a report for the Club of Rome, *The Limits to Growth* (Meadows et al. 1972). The authors modelled the consequences of growing world consumption linked with finite resources. The report was controversial and much criticized. Its message was not liked by policy makers and was largely ignored, as the authors have acknowledged (Meadows et al. 2004). The report predicted that, without major changes of policy, the ecosystem and world economy would collapse in the middle of the twenty-first century. The research was examined again in 2004, finding that the global economy was on the track predicted in 1972 (Meadows et al. 2004). This reinforces the warning that the global economy is on a dangerous trajectory.

The consequences of limits to growth were discussed through the 1970s. Much modern literature is restating these original arguments, so I will lean on the book by Herman Daly, *Steady-State Economics* (1977) to drive home the point that the challenge the world faces is not new insights found through new research; instead, the problem is continued inability, over a period of 40 years, to do anything to change direction, despite the evidence. Herman Daly describes the blinkered view of the economist wedded to the idea of continual growth thus:

> If there is no absolute scarcity to limit the possibility of growth … , and no merely relative or trivial wants to limit the desirability of growth …, then "growth forever and the more the better" is the logical consequence.
>
> (Daly 1977: 41)

In arguing for the concept of a steady-state economy, Daly touches on the issue of population, a recurring theme in the literature going back to Malthus (1826) and used by Daly in his definition of a steady-state economy: 'an economy with constant stocks of people and artifacts, maintained at some desired, sufficient levels by low rates of maintenance throughput' (Daly 1977: 17).

The concept of a steady-state economy did not gain traction, and conventional economists have remained in the driving seat, supporting an expansion in human activity which is now putting the planet under such pressure that a 'perfect storm' is approaching. Climate change, biodiversity loss and rising sea levels and other changes to the planet will hit society hard.

Tim Jackson has brought the limits-to-growth debate up to date in his book *Prosperity without Growth* (Jackson 2009). He provides a clear explanation of the dangers of using growth as the prime aim of policy, and outlines the argument for a prosperous low- or zero-growth economy. Rob Dietz and Dan O'Neill (2013) go further to explore specific strategies to deliver a steady-state economy with the aim of maximizing long-term well-being.

Referring back to Herman Daly's analysis, his summary of the growth challenge remains pertinent today:

> It is a brute fact, however, that there is such a thing as absolute scarcity, and there is such a thing as purely relative and trivial wants. And, if these aspects are dominant at the margin, the implication is the opposite of growthmania, namely, the steady-state economy. Nature does impose an absolute scarcity in the form of the laws of thermodynamics and the finitude of the earth.
>
> (Daly 1977: 41)

> there is really no such thing as equilibrium in an evolving and growing economy. Eventually, growth in real physical production confronts biophysical limits and must stop. Growth in monetary value of financial assets is still possible for a time, but when continued investment of borrowed money drives up value of financial assets more rapidly than the increase in real goods and services, collapse is inevitable, even if we cannot predict precisely when it will occur.
>
> (Daly & Farley 2011: 404)

2.2.2 The rationale for sustainability

A deeper analysis of sustainability follows in Chapter 3. The intention here is to lay some foundations for the research with a set of assumptions. Sustainability has come to mean so many things, is used in so many ways, and applied to so many contexts; that the term on its own has no precise meaning. The rationale for sustainability, as applied in this research, is built on three assumptions:

Assumption 1: Human society has a long-term future

This is an obvious assumption which needs to be stated at this unique point in history. Humans have survived ice ages, plagues and war, and are stronger because of it. Humans now have the technology, knowledge and capability to live better lives than at any point in history, but we are also capable of fundamental modification to the ecosystem on which we depend, which makes it vital that we use our new-found power responsibly. Denial of this assumption, by people who would rather live only for today, undermines the possibility that a stable sustainable global society can be achieved. If such a view were to rule policy, we could be certain that humanity would suffer. Acceptance of the assumption that human society has a long-term future is fundamental to employing the concept of sustainability.

Assumption 2: Successful management of human affairs requires a balance between society, the environment and the economy

Effective sustainable policy should lead to a stable mutually reinforcing balance between, society, environment and the economy. International policy of recent decades has been woefully unsustainable, with worries that unless corrections are made there could be a spiral into mutual collapse (Martenson 2011). The broad nature of the aspirations to improve matters is reflected, at global level, in the United Nations Sustainable Development Goals (SDG). Delivering such a diverse, and in some cases contradictory, range of aspirations for world society is proving difficult (Sach 2015).

Recent work related to sustainability applies the term 'resilience' (Boyd et al. 2008; Hall & Lamont 2013; Brown 2014). This includes the notion that sustainability is not a static state of affairs but to be effective should incorporate a dynamic response and include adaptation by communities to changing circumstances and changes in their external environment. Ron Martin (2012: 2) reports that "'resilience talk" conjures up worries that the notion can all too easily be captured by neo-liberal apologists, to bolster arguments in favour of the need for "flexibility", "self-help" and "competitive fitness"'. It is clear that the concept of resilience is indeed being used to reinforce the neoliberal agenda (Joseph 2013), leading to the danger that it might be used to justify avoiding fundamental change to the economy to limit environmental damage, such as climate change, because resilient people can cope with the consequences

(Hudson 2010; Pelling 2011). Despite such concerns, the idea that effective sustainability should include dynamic adaptation is an important insight.

The world needs sustainable, resilient societies operating in ways that deliver quality of life and protect the ecosystem for now and for future generations. Achieving balanced policy that can match the rhetoric of sustainability is a tough challenge, which becomes even tougher when the constraints of planetary limits are factored into the analysis. The United Nations targets to fight poverty and secure human well-being have to be reconciled with planetary stability (Griggs et al. 2013).

Assumption 3: We live on a finite planet and are totally reliant on its ecosystem services

This is a statement of fact over which there should be no dispute, although policy makers can choose to ignore it or give it scant attention. The assumption here is that in formulating policy for sustainability this fact should be recognized and the consequences for policy accepted.

2.2.3 Planetary limits

> We are using 50 per cent more resources than the Earth can provide, and unless we change course that number will grow very fast – by 2030, even two planets will not be enough.
>
> (Jim Leape, Director General, WWF International, WWF 2012: 6)

The ecological footprint is a measure we can use to compare our consumption of the Earth's resources with its ecological capacity to regenerate (Ewing, Reed et al. 2010). The first set of national ecological footprint accounts relate to 1961 and show that the world was consuming around 50 per cent of its capacity to regenerate (Ewing, Moore et al. 2010:18). At this level, human society was drawing interest on its natural capital without depleting it, a level of consumption that could have continued indefinitely. Half a century later, the human ecological footprint is 150 per cent of the Earth's biocapacity (WWF 2012). This means that we are running down the planet's resources. We can draw down natural capital for some time, but there must come a point when the planet's ecosystem is exhausted – unless we rein back consumption.

2.2.4 Pathways to sustainability

Achieving sustainability, when dealing with the complex dynamic system of the modern world economy, is difficult, particularly when there is considerable uncertainty. Leach et al. (2010) complain that, too often, the response is to look for a blueprint solution to a defined problem when the reality is that negotiating sustainability is a process in which context matters requiring plurality of thinking and diversity of solutions. There are many pathways to sustainability, depending on circumstances, location, resources and capabilities, and these are not static. For sustainability to provide the required stability and resilience, it is unlikely that top-down planning will suffice. A vital ingredient of any solution is local engagement with the challenge and local empowerment towards a dynamic sustainable pathway (Leach et al. 2010). Whatever is proposed to reconcile sustainability and macroeconomic policy, it should enable such dynamic pathways to evolve.

2.2.5 A new definition of sustainability

The assumptions on which this research is built are: that human society has a long-term future; that successful management of human affairs requires a balance between society, the environment and the economy; and that we live on a finite planet and are totally reliant on its ecosystem services. There should be nothing controversial or disputable here. No reasonable person would argue against any of these, except as a debating exercise, but dealing with real policy to address serious existential challenges is not an intellectual debate but part of a real negotiation to secure our future. As such, it requires firm foundations. In the next chapter, this is developed further to craft a working definition of sustainability (McManners 2014: 295): 'Sustainability is the delivery of quality of life in a way that safeguards the global ecosystem for the benefit of future generations.'

The assumptions that underpin this definition may not be contentious, but focussing here when discussing economic policy is controversial, as it leads to confronting the set of assumptions laid out above about economic globalization. Which set of assumptions should have primacy goes right to the heart of the policy challenge.

2.3 Financial crisis of 2008

The financial crisis of 2008 was a significant event for many countries, illustrating the dangers of integrated global finance as financial contagion spread from country to country. Was this a glitch or a symptom of deeper problems? Economist Jagdish Bhagwati wrote in 2004 that at times of financial crisis people question globalization as 'Good times dampen anti-globalization attitudes, while bad times deepen them' (Bhagwati 2004: 10). It is therefore natural that the financial crisis of 2008 should turn sentiment away from globalization. I was one of very few voices who even before the crisis were questioning the probity of globalization. I wrote in a book published before the crisis (McManners 2008: 171–2):

> The flows of capital are increasing, with $1.5 trillion flowing through the currency markets daily, much of it speculative. Cross-border ownerships are increasing. Foreign ownership of US financial instruments in 2005 was:

equities 12%, US corporate bonds 25% and US government bonds 44%. Such global economic interdependence has not been seen before. Is this a strength or a weakness? Is the world financial system a robust self-regulating system or a house of cards waiting to collapse? The amorphous nature of the system makes it hard to judge. It is certainly looking like a system in which we all either stand or fall together. It may be that more connections bring greater resilience and reduce the chances of collapse, but if collapse does come, there will be no hiding from the consequences.

My colleagues in the Business School were dismissive of this view in 2007 when reading advanced copies of the book before publication, but the financial crisis brought to life the doubts I expressed. I was not in fact forecasting an imminent crisis, and my words were more prophetic than I could have expected. My analysis indicated that the crisis had deeper foundations than a cyclical downturn and deserved a stronger response than rebuilding trust in the existing system. The interesting (and concerning) point is that the systemic problems that led to the view I expressed in 2007 remain largely unchanged in 2016. A degree of confidence may have returned but the reasons for caution remain strong. The financial crisis opened people's minds to the possibility that interconnected integrated global financial markets may not be the panacea that many mainstream policy makers were presenting, but following the crisis there remained 'pervasive claims that what we had lived through was simply a temporary blip in a self-correcting free-market system and that what was needed was little more than a perfecting of what was *in situ*' (De Cock et al. 2012).

Focussing on the specific metrics of the crisis in the search for solutions is dangerously myopic. Blame is attributed to sub-prime mortgages in the United States (Financial Crisis Inquiry Commission 2011) and to financial imbalances between the United States and China (Obstfeld & Rogoff 2009). I argue that the underlying cause is deep-rooted systemic problems identified by Richard Barnet and John Cavanagh back in 2001: 'The rise of global financial markets makes it increasingly difficult for national governments to formulate economic policy, much less enforce it' (Barnet & Cavanagh 2001: 67). Their analysis was sound in 2001, and remains sound today, showing greater insight than the numerous post-crisis analyses framed by the simplistic assumption that something in 2008 upset the system.

> Ultimately, change must come in the form of a financial system not based on speculation, but a system that uses funds with geographic roots and some connection with goods and services that cater, as they once did, to the interests of local and regional economies ... Only by such a change in direction can the financial community be remotely in service to ecological and social sustainability.
>
> (Barnet and Cavanagh 2001: 69)

The financial crisis could be a turning point in history, exposing to view the dangers of the current course of human affairs and providing the backdrop for a re-evaluation of macroeconomic policy. This could be a once-in-a-planet opportunity to change the global economy for the better.

2.4 Dilemmas and challenges

This examination of the fault lines between globalization and sustainability has drawn selectively from broad swathes of the literature to build the foundations of a case for change. I could be accused of selecting the evidence that fits my argument but these ideas have been in gestation many years and I believe I have outlined a coherent analysis. I do not take lightly the fact that I dare to question the fundamental basis of international policy and mainstream economics. The research builds on the analysis of the fault lines between globalization and sustainability in the spirit of proposing solutions; the outcome explained in later chapters shows the value of this approach. The dilemmas which need to be addressed are summarized below.

2.4.1 Economic growth and planetary limits

It is natural for all people to desire a better life and better opportunities for their children. Economists have captured the aspirations of the people of the world in a vision of a perpetually growing connected global economy that benefits all, but a market that is not constrained by planetary limits is dangerous.

> The great advantage of the market is that it frees us from concern with the mass of day-to-day allocation problems and allows us to use our limited policy-making capacity to avoid the really big mistakes ... But to trust the market to make decisions that are truly beyond its range can be suicidal. The market cannot, by itself, keep aggregate throughput below ecological limits.
>
> (Daly 1977: 89)

Other writers take a different approach, arguing that free trade may be sensible and necessary to enable the world to live within ecological limits provided national and regional environmental policy is robust and effective (van den Bergh & Verbruggen 1999). The proponents of the Green New Deal seek economic growth through building a greener economy (Barbier 2010). There is also support for the view that the solution is to monetize the environment, putting a value on environmental assets and services (Pearce & Barbier 2000).

The argument that economics should not always dominate policy appears in Dani Rodrik's chapter on 'Growth strategies', with the comment that economists should be employed in their proper capacity as 'evaluators of trade-offs instead of as advocates' (Rodrik 2008: 366). This reinforces Simon Retallack's argument (2006: 314):

Advocates of economic globalization claim that it is instrumental to ecological sustainability on the grounds that it makes environmental protection more affordable and desirable. In reality, however, the natural environment is one of the greatest casualties of economic globalization, which is accelerating the depletion of the planet's natural resource base and the exhaustion of its carrying capacity for wastes at the same time as preventing adequate mitigating action from being taken.

I argue that the danger of not addressing effectively the dilemma between economic growth and the constraints of planetary limits is in a category of risk so severe that the precautionary principle applies (Gollier et al. 2000). Policy makers have yet to admit to this, but the evidence is becoming overwhelming. When this evidence is accepted, and acted upon, the changes that follow will alter how the global economy operates. There will be many changes. An obvious example is managing the relationship between trade and environmental regimes in ways that do not just require the latter to be subordinate to the former (Newell 2002). There will be other changes as finally the global economy is brought back under control to operate within planetary limits.

2.4.2 Technology and policy

No discussion of globalization and sustainability could be complete without touching on the role of technology (Leach et al. 2010). There are many technologies and many associated consequences but the key dilemma seems to be whether the march of technology is outside the control of policy makers, or technology can be harnessed to deliver desirable outcomes. The mainstream view is that Schumpeter's waves of technology are unstoppable and that the process of creative destruction is inevitable, as new technologies displace the old: the car replaces the horse and cart; telecommunications replaces the telegraph; flying replaces passenger liners; and the list goes on (Scherer 1986). A common view amongst economists is that technological advances are generally beneficial. For example, it is a common assumption that technology will find substitutes more quickly than finite resources are depleted so 'finite physical supplies ... are not a large impediment to economic growth' (Jones 2002: 190). Jerry Mander provides an alternative critique, making three main points (Mander 2001: 47).

First, new technologies are presented by those who launch them as improvements and progress.

> It is only long after a technology has entered into general production and has gained an important role in everyday life that we begin to perceive its adverse effects on humans or nature. Even then, the proposed solutions usually consist of creating new generations of technology designed to fix the problems of the old. Thus the wave rolls on to the next technical generation.

Second, 'when we attempt to analyse the virtues of a particular technology, we do so in personal terms … leaving out the social, political and ecological dimensions'.

Third, 'the blinding notion that technologies are neutral … [with] no intrinsic qualities which inevitably produce certain ecological or political outcomes'.

The expanding 'technosphere', as Mander calls it, provides the means to operate an integrated global economy. I regard the rapid movement of information and the potential for improved transparency as intrinsic to the technology of the internet, but the integration of the world economy is a choice we make as to how to use these new means at our disposal. Mander is strident in his criticism of the current trends in technology, arguing that 'the answer is to work to reverse it and bring real power back to local community, while supporting communities, cultures and nations who attempt to stand in the way of the juggernaut' (ibid.). Thomas Kemeny takes a more mainstream approach, explaining the role of technology in globalization thus:

> We therefore have a wealth of suggestive evidence that new technologies are to a significant extent localized in regional agglomerations, as well as in national economies. In the long run, however, individual technologies must cross borders, oceans and continents. Many technologies that rely initially on nonroutine, context-dependent tasks become increasingly standardized and codified. Their geographical specificity is exhausted, and they can be transmitted from place to place at little cost. As technology can be increasingly imitated, rents from it are bid down. Far-flung agents can effectively absorb once localized knowledge, and enter markets for goods that employ them, often competing at a lower cost. Schumpeterian competition is thus replaced by price competition.
>
> (Kemeny 2011: 4–5)

The literature is generally supportive of the view that waves of technology are unstoppable and their role in globalization inevitable, but a few voices, such as Mander, make the important point that technical innovation should be harnessed to deliver human progress rather than be allowed to engulf society. The extent to which policy makers understand and are willing to accept this responsibility is an important aspect of both globalization and sustainability. The view that technology should not be allowed to dictate the direction of human progress is worthy of further exploration, but in this research it will only be touched upon.

2.4.3 Fossil fuel and climate change

For 200 years, the economy has expanded on the back of cheap energy from fossil fuel. Reliance on fossil fuel is engrained in manufacturing, transport and agriculture and reaches into every corner of the economy. The dangers of climate change lead to the simple conclusion that we should stop burning fossil fuel. This is the toughest dilemma in the short term because the disruption will be intense and the outcomes uncertain. The economists do not help much by insisting that alternative energy should not cost more. This is a prime example where policy priorities have become confused and where clarification between the relative importance of economics and sustainability is required. This is a well-defined fault line which is an important thread running through the research. The problem is easy to define but is proving fiendishly difficult to resolve within the current political and economic framework (Helm 2012).

2.4.4 Stability and Instability

The choice between a stable or unstable global economy would appear to require little analysis. Of course a stable global economy would be better, but real stability is not the same as apparent stability. I will attempt to introduce the dilemma, which is examined further in the next chapter. In essence, the issue is this. Globalization is moving towards an interconnected single global economy which, in the short term, provides strong growth and the impression of stability because weakness in one national economy can be countered by leaning for support on the wider global economy. The flaw in this is that such complex capitalist systems are prone to occasional massive collapse (Minsky 1992). Such collapse could extend across the planet if we succeed in building a truly global civilization because, as Martin Jacques (2009) explains, every civilization runs out of steam eventually. An alternative to a global connected economy is a series of more independent economies interacting together (McManners 2010). In such a model, economies could rise and fall relative to each other within a stable macroeconomic framework. This alternative model would require a trade-off between global economic growth and global stability, but until a massive collapse proves that the dangers of globalization are real, it is easier to reap the economic benefits and ignore the risk.

2.5 Conclusions

Fault lines between globalization and sustainability clearly exist, but the precise nature of the difficulties is hard to ascertain from the literature. It is evident that sustainability should be overarching policy but the concept is so all-encompassing that it is difficult to identify the priorities and craft policy that can deliver its broad aspirations. It will be necessary to reframe sustainability with a tighter focus and more specific aims to be able to tie down the challenge. Globalization suffers from a different problem in that its policies are relatively precise, well understood and deeply engrained. The problem with globalization is that it has become an ideology with considerable momentum which is not questioned enough by policy makers to assess whether it continues to have a logical basis. I contend that globalization, as currently implemented by international institutions, is in need of reform, but views are polarized between those who think the model of an integrated global economy needs reinforcing, such as Joseph Stiglitz, and those, such as John Cavanagh (Cavanagh & Mander 2004) and members of the IFG, who think that the model of globalization is fundamentally flawed.

There would appear to be a stalemate, with conflicting viewpoints locked in opposition. There are some commonalities: for example, it is widely recognized that global environmental policy is not working but efforts have tended to focus on improving environmental institutions and negotiating environmental agreements. Where I think there is potential to break the stalemate is to examine the policy framework of globalization in the light of the imperative to deal with global environmental challenges, not as an add-on to economic policy but as the overarching context of policy. Peter Newell made a useful, but not widely recognized, contribution with the suggestion that 'applying the principle of subsidiarity would encourage us to look to regional and national policy-processes as a starting point and only move decision-making upwards when the nature of the problem genuinely requires it' (Newell 2002: 669). I also argue that this approach would be part of the solution but, to succeed, there needs to be a macroeconomic framework that is different to the policies that have brought the world to the current impasse.

The conclusion to this examination of the fault lines at the interface between globalization and sustainability raises some fundamental dilemmas around planetary limits, technology, fossil fuel and economic stability. The questions that arise comprise a high-level and deeply controversial interrogation of the current macroeconomic policy framework. Is economic globalization a Ponzi scheme? If it is, the fundamental basis of the management of international affairs is flawed and needs replacing. Perhaps the situation is not so extreme and globalization can remain as the bedrock of policy. If this is the case, how can it be made to work within planetary limits? If this proves difficult, and there is every indication that this would require an astonishing degree of effective global governance, is there a more pragmatic macroeconomic policy framework that could work? I believe it is prudent to start the search for such a framework, beginning with reframing macroeconomic policy in the context of sustainability, which is the subject of the next chapter.

3 Reframing economic policy towards sustainability[1]

3.1 Introduction

The peoples of the world are rushing headlong into the future, measuring progress by economic growth based on increasing consumption within an increasingly globalized and connected economy. It has become apparent that current policy is failing on many levels: biodiversity loss has accelerated, climate change continues unabated and, despite using economics as the focus of policy, the global economy is struggling. The dire scenario suggested in 1972 – that the economy and the ecosystem may collapse around the middle of the twenty-first century (Meadows et al. 1972 and 2004) – is no longer outlandish. There is a real possibility that civilization is sleepwalking into a terrible crisis (McManners 2009). It is human nature to be optimistic, and not to take doom-mongers seriously, but it would be wise to shift off the current track and onto a safer trajectory.

The idea that sustainability could be the basis of a solution – defined broadly as a balance between the economy, society and the environment – is widely shared, but agreeing a realistic way forward is proving difficult. The time has come to question assumptions and make a fresh start.

The assumption underpinning this chapter is that sustainability is vital to the future of society. There can be little doubt that this is a safe assumption because by definition an unsustainable society has a limited lifespan. Clearly, we want society to continue, so it should be possible to agree that putting sustainability as the foundation of policy is the correct course of action, but the current economy is not sustainable and therefore has to change.

The issue is the need to reform economics to be able to absorb cultural, social and ecological values better. The aim of this chapter is to reframe sustainability as the foundation of this reformed economics, drawing on and adding to the green economics school of thought outlined by Miriam Kennet and Volker Heinemann (2006) in the very first edition of the *International Journal of Green Economics*. First, perspectives on sustainability are examined leading towards the identification of priorities. Second, repositioning economics is discussed to support the development of a set of principles of sustainability economics. Third, the foundations of a sustainable economy are proposed, leading to the immediate and pressing task of replacing the fossil-fuel economy. Finally, brief comment is made on the measurement of success. The analysis presented here touches many issues, so each factor is boiled down to its essence without space to discuss alternative viewpoints. Where this essential brevity has failed to note explicitly the good work of others, I apologize; where I present analysis with which other researchers may disagree, let us have the debate; where I point out some uncomfortable truths, that is the nature of the challenge we must all face together.

3.2 Reflecting on Rio +20

In 2012, the United Nations Conference on Sustainable Development returned to Rio de Janeiro, the location of the 1992 Earth Summit, to review progress. According to Achim Steiner, Executive Director, United Nations Environment Programme (UNEP), the state of the planet, globally and regionally, is 'cause for profound concern' (UNEP 2012).

> Harmful environmental changes are taking place in an increasingly globalized, industrialized and interconnected world, with a growing global population and unsustainable production and consumption patterns. The degradation of ecosystem services is narrowing development opportunities and could threaten future human well-being.
>
> (UNEP 2012: 458)

At the conference, the United Nations Secretary-General's High-Level Panel on Global Sustainability launched their report, *Resilient People, Resilient Planet* (United Nations Secretary-General's High-Level Panel on Global Sustainability 2012). This outlined the challenges of sustainability and reaffirmed plans to deal with them, listing 56 recommendations which 'seek to establish ... a world in which a sustainable, inclusive growth provides more for less, for all'. The report captures a wide range of aspirations continuing the dialogue started in 1987 by the World Commission on Environment and Development (WCED), chaired by Gro Harlem Brundtland, with their report *Our Common Future* (WCED 1987). The dialogue has failed to resolve the crisis over the intervening period of 25 years; it is reasonable to deduce that the dialogue is in some way flawed.

The discussions around sustainability are underpinned by a number of assumptions which, although not stated explicitly, are deeply engrained in the policy silos of world society. From these assumptions discussion takes place and policy options are considered but solutions are proving to be elusive. Perhaps these implicit assumptions are the blockage. In this case it would be useful to bring them to the surface. First, the primary assumption is that neoclassical economics – free markets and assumptions that people make rational choices to maximize their circumstances – remains the bedrock of policy. Second, it is assumed that the changes required will be an evolution from current policy. Third, population growth is assumed to be an unalterable fact. These implicit assumptions should be challenged with the aim of improving clarity and placing sustainability on firm foundations.

Free market fundamentalism is no longer appropriate as the bedrock of economic policy. The world has reached the current impasse partly as a consequence of two decades of feverish defence of the current economic model. The crisis that erupted in 2008 should have exposed blinkered adherence to the conventional economic framework as no longer defensible, but, instead of looking for a change of direction, world policy makers worked at reinforcing the existing system. The High-Level Panel on Global Sustainability argues, 'Achieving sustainability requires us to transform the global economy. Tinkering on the margins will not do the job' (United Nations Secretary-General's High-Level Panel on Global Sustainability, 2012: 9). Quite so, but implicit acceptance of the current economic model eliminates the possibility of transforming the global economy.

In addition to defence of the conventional economic model, there is an implicit assumption that sustainability will be a smooth evolution from the economy and society as it is now. This makes analysis easier because it accepts the reality observed and considers ways to adjust to changing circumstance and altered priorities. This may be convenient, but the assumption of steady evolutionary change filters out potentially valuable solutions. In particular, dealing with fossil-fuel dependency will require a steep change in the way the economy operates. Revolutionary change is disruptive and unpredictable so may not be the policy maker's first choice, but it is not justified to rule out a revolution as the degree of change required and urgency may warrant it (McManners 2008).

A third implicit assumption – which can be a sensitive issue – is population growth. Population is a critical factor in sustainability: the more people, the more their demands and the greater the load on the planet. Population predictions made by the UN should be regarded as indicative of continuing with current policy but not lodged as an unchangeable outcome. Policy that could hold world population in check would obviously make living within the resources of the planet much easier and has such huge potential that it must be part of the solution.

Examination of the Rio +20 process shows that implicit assumptions are holding back consideration of radical solutions. During the 20 years since the Rio Earth Summit, the pace of ecosystem destruction and resource depletion has increased. Instead of renewing efforts to deal with the symptoms, the world needs to rethink its strategy and tackle the cause. Recognizing that discussion has stalled sets the scene for a reappraisal of priorities to lay new foundations of sustainability.

3.3 Perspectives on sustainability

The concept of sustainability impacts every area of policy and every sector of the economy leading to competing interpretations of sustainability (Söderbaum

2008; Gallopín et al. 2014). The universality of the policy is both its strength and its weakness. Sustainability could be the overarching policy framework to which all other policy conforms. On the other hand, if the term 'sustainability' is allowed to morph to fit a wide range of circumstances, it could lose any real meaning.

3.3.1 Development policy

> Sustainable development is development that meets the needs of the present without compromising the ability of future generations to meet their own needs.

This definition has become the prevalent definition of sustainability since it was first put forward by the WCED (1987: 1). The Brundtland Commission's definition was deliberately people-centric, including the concept of 'needs', in particular 'the essential needs of the world's poor, to which overriding priority should be given'. This has been the foundation of policy for development over the last three decades (UNCTAD 2012) but the concept of sustainability now needs to advance to recognize that the planet has limits that have to be respected as an overriding constraint on policy.

The old model of development aid encouraged replication of the economies established in the developed world. The Bruntland Commission is credited with changing the emphasis away from a narrow economic focus to a balance between economic, social and environmental policy. However, the assumption remained that the developed world has the economic model that poorer countries should aspire to adopt, following the same path of industrialization that underpinned the wealth of Western societies. The providers of aid wanted to share their model of success and the receivers of aid were attracted by the apparent benefits. The inherent contradiction, that it would be impossible for people across the globe to live the consumerist lifestyles of a typical European or North American, has been slow to emerge.

In hindsight, it is obvious that the consumption levels of the world's richest economies cannot be replicated widely without stripping the planet bare (Tan & Rose 2007). Idealists have put forward the concept of 'contraction and convergence'. As the poorer countries develop and grow consumption, the rich countries rein back on consumption so that rich and poor converge on an equitable fair share of the planet's resources. This has intellectual appeal but takes little account of political and cultural realities.

A more realistic way forward is based on setting policy that suits the country, its people and its resources. This is a radically different approach, leading to a much wider variety of national policy frameworks. It is not an easy lesson for givers of aid to accept that they should intrude less to encourage sustainability from the bottom up (Glennie 2008).

The term 'sustainable development' arose in the context of aid from world institutions and rich countries to poorer countries according to rich-world assumptions. As sustainability becomes better understood, development policy needs to change in favour of respect for a country's right to build a sustainable society based on their values, their people and their resources.

3.3.2 Government perspective

Governments are beginning to attempt to adopt sustainability as overarching policy (EU 2009b) with limited success (Steurer & Berger 2011). At the national governmental level it has always been necessary to balance economic, social and environmental issues. Finding this balance gets easier as one goes lower down the hierarchy of society to small communities, where it is natural to consider all aspects of policy and broker solutions. At the higher administration levels there need to be explicit linkages which are often lacking or weak. An example of progress is placing climate change and energy policy within the same government ministry, as the UK government decided in 2008 in creating the Department of Energy and Climate Change (DECC). As policy is connected, it should also be balanced, but too often a heavy focus on economic outcomes is allowed to dominate over social and environmental issues. A key problem for national governments is the lack of a framework for sustainability at the international level making it hard for national governments to set sustainable policy.

International policy operates in stovepipes through separate organizations with divergent objectives. For example, the UNEP deals with environmental policy, the IMF focusses on finance, and the WTO on trade. Connections are ad hoc and a global conceptual framework for living within the resources of the planet has yet to emerge. It will become much easier for national governments to set sustainable policy if the world could agree on what comprises macro sustainability. As government struggles to understand what sustainability means from the top down, it becomes very difficult to craft policy and impossible to persuade the electorate of change that alters the status quo. Governments should not delay action to await the emergence of agreement on a concept of macro sustainability but rather seek to understand their global impact as they set national policy concurrent with engaging with efforts to define a global sustainability framework.

3.3.3 Business perspective

The growing awareness and concern about environmental issues within society is forcing industry to take notice (Kolka & Tulderb 2010). Sustainability has become linked with corporate social responsibility as corporations seek to defend the business and safeguard their reputation. This is a reactive approach with corporations focusing on saving costs and selling 'green' products or services. Business will respond to the changing situation but is reluctant to lead substantive change because the commercial parameters are uncertain.

3.3.4 Non-governmental organization (NGO) perspective

Across the NGO community connected solutions under the umbrella of sustainability are seen as the way ahead but, as with government and business, the lack of a coherent global narrative leads to poor coordination and in some cases conflicting actions. Although diversity across the NGO community is often beneficial, with sustainability there needs to be a core narrative to reduce the incidence of contradictory aims and wasted resources.

A broad coalition is emerging that sustainability is important, even necessary, but an agreed model of sustainability is required such that government, business and NGOs can share the same core framework. This framework will necessarily encompass broad swathes of policy but should focus on the skeleton which remains firm whilst the detail is fleshed out through experimentation at the community, national and regional level.

These different perspectives show that the term sustainability is used in a range of contexts and across many areas of research and policy making. For sustainability to deliver on its potential, it has to be reframed and focussed on the key priorities.

3.4 Priorities

The traditional model of sustainability encompasses the economy, society and the environment in one policy framework. Such broad policy requires clear priorities if it is not to become unwieldy and impracticable. This discussion of priorities leads to a tighter definition of sustainability.

3.4.1 Economics

Policy in the modern world is biased towards economic outcomes on the assumption that economic progress is an effective proxy for human progress. It therefore seems natural to start an examination of priorities with the economics of sustainability. The first insight is fundamental, that the established conventional economic framework based on growing the economy and increasing consumption, for all its other merits, is inherently unsustainable. The assumption that economic progress equates to increased human welfare unwinds when the economy comes up against resource limits. Consideration of sustainability exposes a narrow focus on economic objectives as policy with a limited time horizon. Environmental impacts and depletion of non-renewable resources are left outside economic policy and become time bombs waiting for future generations.

Amongst many economists the required response is to bring these missing elements inside the economic framework. Perhaps so, but there is a more fundamental insight, which is that economic outcomes should not in themselves be policy objectives; economics is a tool to deliver policy objectives. This should always have been the case but a focus on economic outcomes has obscured this simple truth.

There is a significant difference between simply bending the current economic framework towards sustainability and recognizing that management of the economy has to be guided by higher policy objectives. The true starting point for teasing out the priorities of sustainability is not economics.

3.4.2 Environment

There is a strong argument that 'environment' should be the main priority of sustainability because whatever else human society achieves we are ultimately totally dependent on a healthy ecosystem. For most of human history, the continuation of ecosystem services was a safe assumption. Human activities were limited in scale and used low technology, so human demands were small compared with the scale of the planet and waste was by default biodegradable. There was no need to respect the limits of the planet, but modern society is of such scale, and has such advanced capabilities, that the planet's natural processes are at risk of damage as planetary limits are breached (Rockström et al. 2009).

The changes inflicted on Planet Earth by human activity are hard to predict with certainty, particularly at the local and regional levels, but what is certain is that we have only one planet. This simple truth is worth stating explicitly to ensure we understand fully that we will have to live with the consequences of the experiments we run. The only safe policy is to respect the limits of the planet to avoid damage to the ecosystem.

The logical deduction is that living within the limits of the planet should be the overriding priority, and that is the foundation of the analysis presented in this chapter. It may be logical but that does not make it easy. In the rich world, there is scope for people to support policy to conserve the planet but the changes required impact lifestyle so there is a difficult political argument to win. In very poor countries, where mere survival is challenging, it is not easy for the poor to adjust to live within planetary limits; people will do whatever is needed to feed their family. Across the world, living within planetary limits in ways that suit the locality and society has to be the prime aim of sustainability policy – otherwise other policy objectives are doomed to fail – but persuading people of the necessity of such policy requires that the social component of policy is given a high priority.

3.4.3 Social provision

In order that a community or society has the capability to play its part in living within planetary limits there needs to be sufficient social provision to ensure that livelihood is safe and secure. Desperate people do desperate things without considering the long-term consequences. People with secure lives are able to consider the needs of future generations, looking at the future through the eyes of their children and grandchildren.

The absolute measure of resources people need to live is small, comprising enough food, enough to drink and shelter. Relative need is much more problematic as people judge what they have in relation to others, initiating a spiral of competitive consumption. It has been shown that increasing income for the very poor leads to increased well-being and happiness, but at higher income levels the correlation breaks down (Layard 2005). People get richer but they do not get happier. Consumption does not bring happiness, so measures of consumption should not be used as a measure of human well-being. Quality of life, not quantity of consumption, should be the aim of social policy. The current economic model, based on increasing production and growing consumption, will have to be reformed if quality of life is to have primacy in economic policy.

3.4.4 Definition of sustainability

The conclusion of this examination of priorities leads to this definition of sustainability:

> Sustainability is the delivery of quality of life in a way that safeguards the global ecosystem for the benefit of future generations.

It is not about quantity but quality in people's lives, within the prime constraint of living within the limits of the planet.

3.5 Repositioning economics

In text books, Adam Smith is credited as being the father of economics. His book, *The Wealth of Nations* (1776) laid out many of the principles of economics that are still used today, but his other great book was *The Theory of the Moral Sentiments* (Smith 1759). Adam Smith was not an advocate of heartless economics based on greed and narrow economic objectives. Writing 200 years ago, he assumed a cohesive and well-ordered society. His ideas were a tool to improve the efficiency of that society; he would be horrified to find that instead of economics serving society, economics has become the master. If Adam Smith were alive today, I believe he would disown the distorted economics of our day and insist that it be brought back to its roots.

A world in which conventional economic models drive policy does not look attractive to a manual worker in the rich world who has lost his job or to a Chinese peasant whose land has been appropriated to build a factory. These are the evident losers of economic globalization, but we are all losers in the dash for growth that ignores the global environmental consequences. Current economic policy has become divorced from the realities of the planet and human society. Fortunately, people are more complex than rational machines simply seeking to maximize short-term personal economic benefits. From a policy perspective, choosing the less than ideal economic choice is seen as weakness, but this is not human frailty so much as human strength to see beyond narrowly defined economic interests.

Economists are inadvertently blocking sustainability by building complex theoretical models and equations that are only intelligible to fellow economists. Policy makers are persuaded to follow the advice of economic advisors without being able to see for themselves through the fog of complexity. Economists can be heard saying words like, 'Whatever is proposed must not cost more or interfere with the principles of free trade.' Such limitations effectively neuter discussion and rule out any realistic resolution of the fundamental issues.

3.6 Principles of sustainability economics

The study of economics seeks to codify complex human society into a framework of numbers and equations. It can only ever be an approximation of reality; and when an economic model fails to match reality, the economic framework should be rewritten. Adherence to the current economic framework has put society on a track that conflicts with higher objectives for the planet and its people. The economic framework therefore needs to be rewritten and existing policy questioned.

It would be presumptuous to suppose that one person, one team or one nation could codify the new economic framework, especially since the framework should be flexible to allow each country to build a sustainable economy that suits its needs, resources and culture. However a common skeleton of principles would be useful to set the foundations of a sustainable economy.

3.6.1 Subservience

The first principle of sustainability economics is subservience to the needs of society and the challenge of living within the limits of the planet. This requires a change in the mindset of policy makers brought up to believe that economics trumps other policy. Some economists might ruffle their feathers at fear of losing primacy in the policy debate but less arrogance and more openness to different economic solutions is how economics can find relevance to the challenges of the twenty-first century.

3.6.2 Control

Economies are inherently complex and chaotic but economic policy needs tools that provide an appropriate degree of control. This should not be a model of central control which is known not to work through examples like the Soviet Union and North Korea. However, recent experience has shown that market fundamentalism with few controls and light-touch regulation is also flawed. An economy without controls is an economy out of control. Even if this economy seems to be doing rather well, it is in danger of crashing with little policy makers can do to prevent it. Policy makers need tools to wield in flexible ways to deliver desired policy outcomes with the reasonable certainty of maintaining macro stability. To work successfully in support of sustainable policy, economic tools should be intelligible to the non-economist, in other words simple and transparent. Complex financial arrangements where the reality is obscured and risk is unknown are not useful. Transparent control mechanisms which provide stability and security are preferable to laissez-faire economic arrangements which may produce greater short-term returns but suffer occasional massive instability and possible collapse.

3.6.3 Balance

Sustainable policy decisions should be balanced to deliver the needs of society in conjunction with sound environmental stewardship using appropriate economic tools. A common method of development is to start with a project proposed on economic grounds; then to consult on the social issues that arise; and finally to commission an environmental impact assessment. Although widely used, this is an unbalanced approach. From an economist's perspective, working with balanced sustainable policy can be frustrating because the most economic solution will often not be the most sustainable solution. This policy reversal will take time to be accepted and embedded in society. For each decision, the issue becomes how to make the most sustainable option economically viable. This is markedly different to seeking to make the most economic solution sustainable.

Rebuilding national economies according to these three principles will lead to a different world economy. Exactly what it looks like will evolve, but almost certainly there will be greater national autonomy and greater variety of national economies as a natural consequence of sustainable policy. This new economy will have different solutions for different countries, which is how it should be, but through the lens of the old economics there will appear to be economic inefficiencies. It will take some time to accept the new thinking. For example, a country that chooses to run a low consumption, agrarian economy adopting objectives such as full employment and a healthy happy population should be free to do so, without outsiders forcing them down the path of industrialization or insisting their markets are opened to cheaper agricultural produce from other countries.

3.7 Foundations of a sustainable economy

The model of sustainability widely employed consists of three pillars of sustainability: the economy, society and the environment. This has been a useful concept to bring these three areas into one model but it also perpetuates the idea that the three are separate. The three are linked, interdependent and cannot stand alone so we need to move onto a model closer to reality. The model proposed here is made not of pillars but of cornerstones to set the shape and structure of the new integrated economy. The cornerstones are:

- culture
- land
- population
- energy.

These cornerstones, and their significance, are discussed below. This approach leads to the following definition of a sustainable economy based on the definition of sustainability provided above:

> A sustainable economy is built upon the cornerstones of culture, land, population and energy to deliver quality of life in a way that safeguards the global ecosystem for the benefit of future generations.

3.7.1 Culture

Culture is at the core of human existence and pre-dates the concept of an economy. Cultures evolve over time to match the circumstances of the community responding to geographic location, availability of resources and history. There are therefore a wide range of cultures reflecting the diversity of the geography of the planet. For example, the culture of the United States derives from its relatively recent expansion as settlers from Europe advanced across a continent of apparently limitless resources from the East to the West coast across thousands of miles of virgin territory. This culture has built a powerful country and a strong economy but it is not a culture appropriate for countries with different circumstances.[2]

In Europe, the fault lines in the euro zone can be traced back to the culture clash between the Mediterranean countries, in which society norms derive from a benign climate where quality of life is perhaps easier to achieve, and the countries of northern Europe, where a more disciplined approach derives from the need to survive a long harsh winter. These cultural differences are not only part of the vibrancy and wonderful diversity of the European community but also have a purpose so society can adjust to its circumstances. Attempting to override culture to implement the perceived economic benefits of a single currency has proved difficult and conflicts with sustainable policy. It may be that European countries will converge politically to a federalist structure, as many policy makers champion, but forming the single currency in advance of the political and cultural shift has been problematic. Retaining cultural diversity, which reinforces the connection between a society and its geography and circumstances, is not simply the preservation of heritage (Jacoby & Cooper 2012) but a necessary part of macro sustainability (McManners 2010: 108).

The adoption of economics at the core of policy has not only tended to overlook culture, but has also had cultural implications as the economic assumption of maximizing behaviour has taken hold. Educating people in modern economics encourages people to be greedy and put self-interest first so that this becomes normal, even expected behaviour.

Sustainability requires a culture based on quality of life (not quantity) and valuing community above self. These are common attributes of long-standing cultural norms which survive into the modern world when people do what they feel is right. Altruism and selfless behaviour do not fit the conventional economic model but society would be a dull and dangerous place without such cultural hangovers.

The economy that suits a particular country is closely linked with the culture that pertains. Imposing economic policy packages across cultural boundaries is not sensible, and not sustainable. A prime example is the Washington Consensus policies widely recommended as the 'best' policy package for a modern economy; this prescriptive approach often fails to deliver as intended in different national contexts (Gore 2000). The culture of a society should be respected and economic policy selected to fit. Economic policy should not be dictated by people from outside the country with a different cultural background and influenced by different experiences of resource availability.

3.7.2 Land

When the human population was small the continents of the world seemed like a limitless resource, but it is now clear that land is a finite resource and a fundamental constraint on society and the economy.

The monetary value of land is based on the income that can be derived from it. Urban land is the most valuable, able to command a high rent; agricultural land is the next most valuable category because it produces cash crops; land left for nature has no monetary value within the conventional economic system.

Sustainability values this resource differently, as land is vital to the stability and security of the global ecosystem. Nature reserves are a part of the solution but it is not enough to have isolated enclaves of biodiversity if the economy is allowed free rein to maximize the value of the surrounding land. The result would be a checkerboard of concrete and intense agriculture. Sustainable land policy requires corridors connecting nature reserves, rebuilding biodiversity within agriculture and encouraging nature back into cities. Agriculture becomes a vital business, not just to produce food efficiently but also to increase the resilience of the ecosystem.

The economic consequences of sustainable land use policy include acceptance that sufficient land is kept out of the economy as a permanent home for nature. The economic framework also has to support sustainable farming and facilitate drawing biodiversity into the spaces occupied by humans. This is vital to protection of the ecosystem, but fortunately is also a way to increase quality of life. Ways have to be found to bend economics away from simple exploitation to a complex system of land management that delivers what humans need and that conserves the ecosystem.

The economics of land should be subservient to sustainability, controlled through legislation and balanced between the categories of urban, agriculture and nature. Mechanisms like an urban–eco balance tax (McManners 2010) can use economics to facilitate linking human needs with the needs of nature to reintegrate society as an integral part of the ecosystem. Land is not simply a means to derive an income but the basis of human survival and the economic framework needs to be carefully crafted to preserve its true value, which is not captured in monetary terms.

3.7.3 Population

The dialogue about sustainability is easier if the issue of population is avoided; but unless the issue of population is treated as one of the cornerstones of policy, the structure will surely fail. The more people drawing on a resource pool, the less available for each person. The reverse corollary is that the fewer people for any given resource pool, the more available for each person. Living within the limits of resources correlates directly with population.

Load on the planet = population x consumption

This simple equation is the most important equation in the economics of sustainability. As the world population expands, and individual consumption climbs, the load on the planet increases. Already humans are consuming 150 per cent of the ecological capacity of the planet (Global Footprint Network 2012) and the upward trajectory continues. To live within the limits of the planet, either population has to reduce or individual consumption diminish, or both.

Economic globalization has encouraged the idea that open global markets will always provide enough, undermining the natural process of communities finding balance between population and available resources. Society has developed complex ways to hold population in check as people observe the opportunities for their children and plan accordingly, but these informal methods are undermined when the link with resources is severed.

Sustainable policy requires focussing on population, with each country crafting population policy appropriate to its circumstances. In developing countries, where the challenge is most intense, this is likely to include improved care for the old (so people do not need large families for a safe old age) and education for girls so that women know how to limit their fertility and have career options other than child rearing. In developed countries it may suffice to alter the tax and benefit system to include disincentives to having more than two children.

There are economic consequences of population policy. First, rising population is not the benefit that conventional economists report when using the language of rising GDP, increasing number of workers and more consumers. Rising population is an increasing liability to provide resources over people's lifetime from birth through working age to retirement. An example is India with its expanding population, which is often reported in terms of its growing workforce and associated increasing influence in the world economy. In reality,

India has a huge looming problem to feed the aspirations of these people in a world of tight resources. Population has the economic characteristics of a liability, not an investment. Second, sustainable population policy leads to an ageing population as governments find they can squeeze the birth rate lower combined with healthcare improvements leading to people living longer. Through the tunnel vision of conventional economics, it can be argued that ageing population is dealt with by encouraging immigration and providing incentives to increase the birth rate. The first principle of sustainability economics is that economics is subservient to the needs of society. Sustainable economic policy has to embrace the demographic shift to an ageing population, not seek to prevent it.

Sustainable economic policy for population recognizes population as a liability, seeks to hold population in check, and embraces an ageing population as integral to the new economy.

3.7.4 Energy

The most unbalanced policy within the global economy is energy, where long-standing reliance on fossil fuel has both distorted the economy and become a threat to the ecosystem. Another cornerstone of sustainable policy is therefore energy.

It is clear that fossil-fuel dependency must end, either because supplies run low or because the consequences for the climate are so severe that people will no longer tolerate its use. Sustainable policy requires deciding the sustainable solution and targeting economic policy to deliver it. The sustainable solution is to dismantle the fossil-fuel infrastructure and replace it with a low-carbon infrastructure within a timeframe that prevents serious damage to the ecosystem. If the warnings from the 1970s oil crisis had been heeded, we could now be living in an economy less dependent on oil.[3] But it was not understood at the time that environmental risk increased the gravity of the situation. Now that we fully understand the problem, it is urgent to use policy to force an early transition.

The modern economy is heavily dependent on fossil fuel, with coal used widely to generate electricity and oil for transport systems, as well as feedstock for plastics and fertilizers. Immediate withdrawal of fossil fuel would collapse the economy.

The cost of fossil fuel is the source of the long-standing problem because the economy has developed on the assumption that energy is cheap. For example, instead of constructing buildings designed carefully to fit the climate, architects put forward designs knowing that systems can be bolted on to heat or cool the building as required. The transport infrastructure has expanded to include the air freight of vegetables between continents because it is affordable. Farmers boost output using industrial practices and fertilizer derived from fossil fuel, rather than manage the complexities of sustainable farming, because these inputs are cheap.

The fossil-fuel economy is not sustainable but it is deeply engrained and no one alive today has experience of a different economy. The global fossil-fuel economy has also unbalanced the world financial system with huge capital flows to oil-producing countries. As demand outstrips supply, these capital flows will increase. Consuming countries are building up long-term debt to keep the fossil-fuel economy running, taking cash out the economy that could be invested in building the economy beyond oil. The countries represented by the Organization of the Petroleum Exporting Countries (OPEC) increase production to keep oil affordable and defend their unsustainable position for as long as possible. Producers and consumers of oil are locked into an outdated economic model that preserves the status quo. Replacing the fossil-fuel economy is the most challenging aspect of sustainability economics.

3.8 Replacing the fossil-fuel economy

Until recently, the CO_2 emitted as a by-product of burning fossil fuel did not have cost implications. This anomaly was not exposed because CO_2 is not a pollutant in the normal sense but a component of the natural processes of the planet. The problem is not CO_2, but the excess of CO_2 in the atmosphere, which is at record levels and continuing to climb. The solution requires concerted action to rein in the global fossil-fuel economy.

For over 200 years, on a project-by-project basis, the infrastructure of the modern world has been built predicated on cheap fossil fuel. Over the next few decades this infrastructure will have to be withdrawn and replaced on a project-by-project basis with low-carbon technology. There is ample renewable energy[4] from the sun, the wind and tides but harvesting it is harder (and more expensive) than extracting easy oil and coal. Energy in a sustainable economy will therefore cost more – perhaps substantially more – supporting not just renewable energy harvesting but also forcing frugal use of energy to peg costs.

Conventional economics leads to the often-quoted metric that for renewable energy to be viable it must cost less than coal. This is another example of a blockage to sustainable policy put in place by economists.

The sustainable solution is to dismantle the fossil-fuel economy and replace it with a low-carbon economy. The economic tool that can be employed to deliver this high-level policy objective is to increase the price of fossil fuel on a steep upward trajectory according to a timetable published in advance to give firm foundations to investment decisions. Overall, energy will cost more and the economy will have to adjust; in many cases limiting overall costs through a step change in energy efficiency.

Leaving it to the market price of fossil fuel would also eventually drive change but, as supplies are constricted, the increased cost would be transferred to the treasuries of oil-rich countries. Governments would find it very hard to invest in low-carbon public infrastructure and support improvements in the energy efficiency of the housing stock. Pre-emptive government action could keep oil prices low through the transition as demand is choked off faster than supplies are depleted. This seems counterintuitive within current norms of economic policy, where it is assumed that high oil prices will drive change, but it would be possible, with sustained and effective demand reduction, to hold oil prices down, thus retaining more cash within national economies. Driving fossil-fuel prices high with government taxes whilst holding oil prices low may be politically difficult, but is such a benign economic scenario for governments that it is worth pursuing.

It will take decades to replace the physical infrastructure of the fossil-fuel economy but the conceptual economic framework can be provided almost overnight. The economic policy to deliver the transition to renewable energy is taxation of fossil fuel escalating to a level that fossil fuel is driven out of the economy using the tax receipts to invest in the low-carbon economy.

This conceptually simple solution leads to a complete reconfiguration of the economy – which is exactly what is needed. However, policy makers discuss ever more complex economic tools around incentives and carbon markets on the false premise that fossil fuel can be replaced by renewable energy at a similar cost, leaving the economy largely intact. This denial of reality is leading us into a drawn-out and painful transition in which climate change becomes a serious problem. The sustainable solution leads us into a short and very painful transition that puts us in a better position sooner. Fossil-fuel dependency is a seriously dangerous addiction; the pain of curing it cannot be avoided and should be faced without further delay.

3.9 Measuring success

Growth in GDP is used widely by government as a prime measure of progress but it is not a measure of the health of society. The inventor of Gross National Product (GNP), the predecessor of GDP, said of his creation that, 'The welfare of a nation can scarcely be inferred from a measure of national income' (Kuznets 1934). Simon Kuznets's words are as true now as when he wrote them. More recently, Tim Jackson explains that growth in GDP is not a necessary route to prosperity (Jackson 2009). GDP is not, and perhaps never has been, a good measure of progress.

There is a management theory adage that what gets measured gets managed. Relevant measures for society should include health, well-being, security and other measures directly related to quality of life. Other important measures relate to the stability and health of the ecosystem. Figures for biodiversity loss and carbon dioxide levels in the atmosphere should be ringing alarm bells across the planet with policy makers rushing to make adjustments to policy. Instead, policy makers worry more about maintaining growth in GDP. There could not be a clearer example of the wrong measure producing the wrong behaviour.

The exact mix of metrics to gauge quality of life and ecosystem integrity will need to be worked on (Bartelmus 2009 and 2010) but the first task is simple: to stop using GDP as an objective of policy. Economic policy should be judged on how well it delivers sustainability objectives for land, population and energy. This would provide the tight clear focus that the world needs at this important juncture in world history.

3.10 Conclusion

Ensuring the sustainability of human affairs is vital to the future of society. Current policy is deeply unsustainable with a narrow focus on economic objectives being part of the problem. However, economics has powerful tools to apply to finding solutions, provided there is willingness to rethink the basis of the economic models.

To make economics relevant to the twenty-first century, it needs to be repositioned to be subservient to the needs of society and compliant with effective stewardship of the ecosystem. Sustainability economics is about control and balance, rather than laissez-faire free markets.

The objectives of economic policy need to match sustainability objectives, respecting the positive role that culture plays in national policy to help communities to adjust to local circumstances. A fundamental objective of policy is to maintain a balance in the use of land which allows the ecosystem to continue providing ecosystem services without interruption. Holding population in check is another fundamental policy objective. Economic policy has to bend to support these high-level objectives.

The area where the economy is most distorted, and where urgent reform is required, is energy policy. An alternative economic framework for sustainable energy could be put in place immediately, to initiate the transformation that will take decades to complete. The replacement of the fossil-fuel infrastructure will be slow but must start without further delay. The conventional economic view has to be recognized as a block to progress to allow enlightened economists the space to develop solutions.

Economics is in the dock for its role in taking the world into a crisis of our own making. Economics can be our salvation, but not through application of conventional economics as we know it. A renaissance in economics is possible but, as Edward Fullbrook (2010) argues, neoclassical economics has to be challenged to make way for new economic models. Many blocks of economic policy will survive but need to be repositioned around the cornerstones of sustainability to provide the integrated model required to steer human affairs out of the current crisis and onto a safe track.

Notes

1   This chapter was first published in the *International Journal of Green Economics* (McManners 2014).
2   The modern culture of the United States, which has been so successful until now, replaced the indigenous culture of the Native Americans who had deep respect for their place within the natural world. The United States now faces the challenge of rediscovering this respect and melding it with modern aspirations.

3 The oil crisis of the 1970s exposed the risks of reliance on foreign oil and started a transition to other energy sources but when the crisis ended oil supplies looked secure (and cheap) and the transition stalled. Infrastructure tends to be replaced within a 40-year cycle so if the move away from oil, considered in the 1970s, had been followed through we could now be living in an economy no longer dependent on oil.

4 It would be hard, if not impossible, to deliver the same quantity of energy we draw from the wasteful use of cheap fossil fuel, but there is ample renewable energy for an appropriately configured sustainable economy.

4 The action research case study approach

A methodology for complex challenges such as sustainability in aviation[1]

4.1 Introduction

The context of the research reported here is an investigation into how to embed sustainability within policy. Aviation was selected because it is widely regarded as one of the most difficult areas of application of sustainability (Nijkamp 1999; Gössling & Upham 2009). Here the focus is on the interface between economic and environmental policy requiring trade-offs between, on the one hand, the benefits of fast affordable transport facilitating trade and tourism, and on the other, the drawback that this is the source of CO_2 emissions implicated in causing climate change. The 'action research case study' proved to be effective in this context and could be useful in other studies which have similar characteristics.

Aviation has come a long way since the first sustained powered flight by the Wright Brothers in 1903. It was propelled by a simple and inefficient engine they had built themselves. For one flight, on one day, over a century ago the pollution hardly mattered. Since that day, aviation has moved forward in leaps and bounds and now provides a high capacity and reliable global air transport infrastructure. The aircraft are vastly better and the aviation industry is hugely successful in connecting people and acting as an enabler for the global economy.

Alongside this success there is the downside of CO_2 emissions, an issue which is only now moving to centre stage as concern over climate change grows. Despite improvements in engine and aircraft design, jet aircraft are inherently energy intensive machines. Aviation now accounts for 2–3 per cent of global CO_2 emissions. These emissions are set to rise in line with growth in aviation capacity, which has been running at over 4 per cent annually since 1989, and expected to continue to grow at a similar rate up to 2030 and beyond (Preston et al. 2012).

The future of aviation has become a highly polarized debate between the environmental movement and an informal alliance of government, industry and passengers (SDC 2007; Daley 2010). An environmentalist view is that aviation stands out like a sore thumb, pouring out emissions at a time when the evidence is clear that man-made CO_2 emissions are causing climate change (Watson 2014). Meanwhile the aviation industry has responded to pressure to reduce emissions by proposing aspirational targets (ICAO 2010a). However, advances such as improvements in jet aircraft efficiency are eclipsed by the overall growth in global air transport capacity. The majority view tends towards defence of the current state of affairs, with most mainstream policy analysts, politicians and business people agreeing that aviation is vital to the economy and a key facilitator of international trade (Hummels 2007). The research showed that currently passengers also tend towards passive defence of the status quo, liking the speed, ease and affordability of flying. A debate about sustainability and aviation policy has started in the UK but the mindset does not yet exist, at national or international level, to take effective and substantive action (Gössling & Upham 2009).

The research had two primary aims: first, to identify a way forward for sustainability in the aviation sector; second, to discover insights into the challenge of implementing sustainable policy which might be applicable, not just in aviation, but also in other sectors and other areas of policy. This chapter focusses on the research process, outlining the phases of the research, explaining the process, and reflecting on what worked well, what didn't and any relevant insights into the research process. It begins with outlining what is an action research case study, leading into a detailed description of the methodology employed. The three phases of the research are explained, starting with the preparatory phase followed by the second phase searching for ideas from another sector with similar characteristics. The third phase was the main empirical research consisting of a series of 28 interviews across six stakeholder groups. Discussion of the analysis is presented and the findings outlined before closing with the conclusions. First, let us consider why action research was selected as the research methodology.

4.2 Action research

As the methodology was being considered, it became clear from the nature of the problem that it would require an amalgam of research methods. A useful pointer from the literature was that the method should be designed to suit the research objectives rather than a hammer applied indiscriminately (Poteete et al. 2010). The potential of action research to be instrumental in the movement for a sustainable world has been recognized (Gustavsen 2008). It has also been used with regard to mobilizing grassroots action to influence climate policy (Hall et al. 2010). The notions of critical pragmatism and deliberative practice (Forester 2013) were also relevant in this case. Previous research into sustainability in aviation had failed to go much beyond identifying the nature of the challenge and proposing marginal changes. There seemed little point in repeating a similar process; it was felt that the research method needed to be more incisive, to go deeper, to challenge assumptions and to take an activist approach. Action research therefore seemed to provide a suitable methodological umbrella under which to build the specific research process.

The attraction of action research is summed up by the editor of *Action Research* writing, 'Action Research is not a method, but an orientation to inquiry' (Bradbury 2013: 3). Hilary Bradbury recommends a working definition of action research (Reason & Bradbury 2000: 1) which focusses on the investigation of social phenomena. It may seem odd to apply the methodology in this case, in what amounts to a macroeconomic challenge, but on examination this is not so odd at all. The economic policies adopted arise from the social interaction between economists, politicians and others. Part of the problem is that economics is considered to be superior to other policy; it is only through mediation that the acceptance of other priorities can be brokered. It is suggested that solving current challenges at the interface between economic and environmental policy may boil down to solving the social challenge of persuading people to accept deep-rooted change to contemporary value systems currently based on a narrow economic outlook.

4.3 The action research case study

The intention was to take an action research approach to carrying out a case study into aviation. To ensure academic rigour, an established case study methodology was employed using the procedures defined by Robert Yin (2014). Initially, this structured case study methodology appeared to contradict the notion of a flexible action-orientated approach. It became clear through the conduct of the research that clear structure was actually a help rather than a hindrance, provided it was applied in support of the action-orientated inquiry. The analogy of scaffolding rather than a cage comes to mind; the two might have a similar look but their purpose is quite different.

In crafting the process of the action research case study, care is needed to ensure it is sufficiently rigorous and can be defended as reliable research. In action research it is hard for the researcher to remain neutral (McNiff & Whitehead 2000). A key challenge is to ensure that the research component is sufficiently rigorous without sacrificing relevance (Argyris & Schön 2005). Such dangers cannot be eliminated entirely but the structured approach followed in this research underpins the integrity of the research process.

The general notion of action research, to determine real-world solutions to real-world problems, is attractive but what specifically is an action research case study? A tight prescriptive definition could inhibit further development (Altrichter et al. 2002), but a definition is offered that gets to the heart of what is different about the action research case study:

> An action research case study employs an action orientated approach to a prescriptive case study process combining problem solving with research in a way that is appropriate to the circumstances of the research to provide both academic rigour and practical relevance.

It is argued here that such action research is particularly relevant to the resolution of conflicted policy at the interface between the value systems of the environmentalist and the economist. The degree of distrust and potential for misunderstanding requires that the researcher fully engages with understanding the opposing viewpoints to be able to propose solutions. There are parallels with arbitration services where the arbitrator is careful to be neutral but also needs to understand and be respected by the parties on both sides of the dispute. A neutral observer would achieve little; a successful arbitrator has to develop a deep understanding of the problem and competing viewpoints to be able to formulate and propose a solution. The parallel with arbitration is not exact but the analogy helps to explain and justify the approach taken in this research. The intention was to become an objective participant and develop ideas to feed back to the subjects of the research and to test their validity within a robust research framework.

4.4 Methodology

The methodology was designed with the intention of getting inside the industry and its network of stakeholders to develop a visceral understanding of the issues. Whereas most research and consultancy is carried out by an outsider looking in, in this case, the objective was to mimic the role of an insider (Coghlan & Brannick 2000). It was hoped that the methodology would allow the research to benefit from both perspectives: the insight that comes with close engagement and the objective view of arriving new to the issues.

Phase 1 was a comprehensive analysis of aviation, and international aviation policy, including previous research focussed on aviation and sustainability. The objective was to identify the key parameters of how the industry operates, including the main issues and potential fault lines in policy, as well as to start to outline possible ways forward. Comprehensive preparatory work in this phase would allow the empirical research to be incisive and focussed on searching for solutions.

Phase 2 was about seeking ideas from a related sector facing similar challenges, in this case the car industry. The aim was to collect insights from a parallel perspective which could be useful in the research and help in crafting the protocol for the Phase 3 research.

Phase 3 was the main empirical research consisting of 28 interviews across six stakeholder groups. The research protocol for this drew heavily on well-established case study methodology (Yin 2014). The protocol was crafted with the subsequent analysis in mind to ensure the data was collected with a structure that would make the analysis more straightforward than it would otherwise be.

4.5 Phase 1: preparatory research

The aim of the preparatory phase was to enter the action research with a comprehensive and accurate picture of business as usual and a vision of a low-carbon future. Developing the latter was not entirely straightforward in a complex industry where the current approach to sustainability is somewhat opaque. In this phase, the notion that drives the process is to establish the groundwork for the researcher to be able to wear a number of hats to empathize with a variety of stakeholders without taking ownership of any one hat.

In this case, aviation is a highly regulated industry with the overarching policy framework overseen by the International Civil Aviation Organization (ICAO), a UN agency created in 1944 on the signing of the Convention on International Civil Aviation (Chicago Convention). The convention covers everything from airport design and air traffic control to aircraft noise and aviation fuel specifications (ICAO 2006). The environmental impact of aviation is well documented, particularly with regard to emissions at ground level close to airports (Stettler et al. 2011). There are also documents explaining the impact of CO_2 emissions in the context of climate change including long-term and short-term effects (e.g. Lee et al. 2010). The viewpoint of environmentalists is captured in a number of books following the general thrust of recommending flying less or not at all (Bridger 2013; Watson 2014). The economic aspects of the current model are also well documented (O'Connor 2001; Holloway 2008; Vasigh et al. 2010). Interestingly, the environment did not feature in these textbooks of aviation economics, even though the economic impact when policy makers start to deal seriously with emissions will be significant. Quite why the aviation industry and its economic advisers have not factored in emissions reduction measures was an interesting point to test in the empirical research. The UK aviation industry's approach to sustainability was documented by the industry organization Sustainable Aviation with documents such as their CO_2 Road-Map (Sustainable Aviation 2012) and Sustainable Fuels UK Road-Map (Sustainable Aviation 2014). There were also reports of previous analysis of sustainability in aviation (Gössling & Upham 2009; SSEE 2010; McManners 2012).

The output from the preparatory research phase was a clear understanding of continuation of business as usual and a scenario 'low-carbon future'.

4.6 Phase 2: seeking ideas

In addition to the preparatory research focussed on the case under the analytic microscope, it proved useful to develop a parallel perspective from a different sector. The aim was to arm the action researcher with ideas to apply in the main empirical research.

This parallel perspective was gathered from a half-day in-depth exploratory interview with an entrepreneur applying an ambitious and uncompromising sustainability agenda within the car industry. This sector of ground transportation has some similarities with aviation, dominated by big corporations and heavily dependent on petroleum fuels. Like aviation, there is inertia within an industry where levels of investment are high and there are strong commercial reasons to defend the status quo. Within the car industry it is considered likely that the hydrogen fuel cell will be the basis for propulsion in the long future but not in the near term. This entrepreneur was taking the view that the hydrogen fuel cell could be deployed much sooner than the industry was expecting, and he was pushing back against industry assumptions in driving his business forward.

One insight from the car industry was the crucial role that government has in supporting the introduction of new technologies. Another useful insight was that care must be taken not to be blinkered by the current industry model, seeking only to insert and replace individual elements. The research has to examine the whole system and consider the possibility of systemic change. For example, the entrepreneur in ground transportation had not defined his business as building cars but the purpose was, 'To pursue, systematically, the elimination of the environmental impact of personal transport'. The words are illustrative of openness to solutions other than the car. The action research case study would not therefore focus on the sustainability of each element – the current approach to sustainability in aviation – but on a complete sustainable low-carbon model for air transportation.

There was considerable value arising from this loosely structured discussion about a related sector before embarking on the case study, as it sparked ideas without the risk of compromising the rigorous research process applied to this particular case study. In the general case, it would be worthwhile to search through the growing body of literature on 'sustainable transitions' (Markard et al. 2012) to discover insights into what has worked in other cases and other sectors.

4.7 Crafting the case study protocol

The intense preparatory work established a solid foundation and structure for the action research. The analysis had defined the current aviation model, traced the historic path it had followed and explored how aviation could change in response to concerns about CO_2 emissions. From this foundation, a particular scenario, 'low-carbon future', had been developed to be put forward and tested on its merits. It was not claimed that this was a precise prediction of the future but it showed that sustainable aviation is feasible. Stakeholders interviewed were much more willing to engage in a discussion about change when presented with a positive alternative rather than one focussed simply on curtailing air transportation. This vision of the future was used to explore whether people could be persuaded to embrace change and the steps required to realize it. The action researcher had in effect become an advocate for a particular model of change, but care was needed that this advocacy did not compromise objectivity. This is where the case study protocol was important in providing a structured framework for the research. The protocol was structured to ensure that the proposal was 'presented' rather than 'sold', allowing people space to give their view freely.

4.8 Phase 3: the main empirical research

The plan for the main empirical research was to engage with stakeholders on a one-to-one basis, probing, testing and challenging views. The stakeholders were selected across six stakeholder groups, as shown in Table 4.1.

The aviation industry was broadly defined to include airlines and aircraft manufacturers. For this group and governmental stakeholders, it was decided to target people with either a direct interest or some knowledge of sustainable aviation so that they would have the insight to make a substantive contribution. Similarly, stakeholders drawn from industry outside aviation were chosen where air transportation was important to their business so they would have strong interest in the research. For passengers, the selection was made to cover a range of socio-economic groups. An issue that emerged from the research was potential unfairness of policy which would restrict the choices for less affluent people; therefore a passenger sub-group was formed of 'package holiday passengers'. Environmentalists were selected from across a broad range and not just those known to be hostile to aviation.

Some interviewees could be a member of more than one stakeholder group. For example, one of the package holiday customers worked as an air traffic controller so he had good insights into both the aviation industry and passenger perspectives. It was decided that in such cases the interviewee could belong to a primary and a secondary stakeholder group. A further classification was added as the research progressed of 'potential change maker'. These were people with a seniority or role with the potential to influence the future of aviation. It was useful to identify these people to gauge their willingness to, and the likelihood that they might, lead change and what it might take to persuade

Table 4.1 Interview and stakeholder table structure

Stakeholder Groups (SG):			Additional Stakeholder Group:		
Aviation Industry (AV)			*Potential Change Maker (CM)*		
Passenger (PASS)					
Environmentalist (ENV)					
Governmental (GOV)					
Industry (not aviation) (IND)					
Package Holiday Passenger (PACK)					
Interview	*Primary SG*	*Secondary SG*	*Name*	*Organization*	*Date*
1	AV				
2	GOV	CM			
3	ENV				
4	PASS				
5	IND				
6	GOV				
7	PACK	AV			
8	AV				

them to do so. These people were a Member of Parliament, the Chief Executive of an aviation industry body, a Chief Scientist to one of the government departments, a member of the UK Committee on Climate Change and a key government official.

From the preparatory research a number of propositions had been extracted (37 in total). These were placed within a nested hierarchy of primary, secondary and tertiary propositions. An example of a proposition and stakeholder reactions is shown in Exhibit 1.

Exhibit 1: Stakeholder reactions to proposition 1.1.8

1.1.8 Current passenger attitudes will not embrace curtailing the availability of affordable flights.

Package holiday passenger

I think someone could put a case forward to the human rights thing saying we have been disadvantaged.

Aviation industry

It is obviously cheap fares that allow the growth of aviation. That is the driving force behind growth in aviation, cheap fares. If you put fares up, you can go back to making it the preserve of the rich, business and wealthy.

Environmentalist

I think the public good would be served by curtailing the availability of all flights, affordable and expensive.

Government

The way that you improve the sustainability of the environment is to price people out of taking flights; I don't think that is realistic.

There were also 'alternative propositions' which equated to Robert Yin's 'plausible rival explanations' (Yin 2014: 140). These were not supported by robust evidence but were put into the same rigorous process to be tested. An example of an alternative proposition is 'The difficulties in finding an alternative to the current model of aviation are so great that it should be accepted as a special case for exemption.' This was noted in the literature but not supported (Ekins & Speck 1999). However, it was tested in the empirical research and produced very interesting results. First, there was near universal agreement, even from those inside the industry, that this was a false proposition. Second, in almost every interview it was stated that someone else should take the lead. The key insight from examination of this alternative proposition was the lack of ownership of the challenge. So feeding alternative propositions into the empirical research is not just an important check on the research process but can also produce useful additional insights.

The interview questions were then designed to test the propositions. Both the propositions and alternative propositions were put into a matrix cross-referenced with the interview questions and the stakeholder groups (see Table 4.2). Not all propositions were relevant to all stakeholders so different interview plans were generated for each stakeholder type, with the wording of the specific question designed to test the proposition within that stakeholder group. Some questions were designed to test more than one proposition. The interviewer had the freedom to alter the question to suit the stakeholder and to ask additional questions to tease out deeper insights. This meant that despite the tight structure, the interviewer could build empathy with the interviewee by asking questions in a way that suited them. The dialogue with an environmentalist, for example, developed quite differently to someone in the aviation industry even though many of the same propositions were being explored.

This structured approach was rigorously applied, which gave consistency across interviews despite the considerable variety in the outlook and scope of the interviews. Building the research protocol in this way was time consuming but the time expended was recouped in the analytic stage because the data already had a clear structure supporting drawing together insights from all the interviews relating to each proposition: for example, the proposition: 'cost-conscious travellers would be willing to sacrifice speed of travel to keep costs affordable'. When all the data was collated the conclusion was that leisure passengers would sacrifice speed of travel to keep costs affordable, whilst business passengers would pay the premium to travel fast. A view from an aviation industry stakeholder was that 'once passengers had done it once or twice they would be happy'. A key insight was that a better quality experience would diffuse concern over a longer journey time. Such collation and analysis was repeated for all 37 propositions. Overall, this was an efficient and effective

Table 4.2 Interview matrix (showing propositions linked to questions and stakeholder)

Question	Prop. (e.g.)	Stakeholder group					
		Aviation industry	Passenger	Environ-mentalist	Govern-mental	Industry (not aviation)	Package holiday passenger
1	1.3.2	X	X	X	X	X	X
	2.3	X			X	X	
2	3.1			X			

method but required care in the way it was conducted to ensure that the structure was supportive of drawing out the most from the interview rather than a straitjacket limiting people's response.

As the interviews were carried out, immediate reflection after the interview was used to confirm whether the research protocol could be improved or should be adjusted. The most significant change arising from this was an adjustment to the planned stakeholder groups in response to the emerging issue of the potential inequity of policy that limited affordable flying for the general public. It was therefore decided to form a sub-stakeholder group of package holiday customers.

4.9 Interviews

The interviews were structured in three parts. First, attitudes to, and opinions about, the current model of aviation were explored. Second, possible changes and improvements were discussed. Finally, the interview looked to the future including putting forward the alternative model 'low-carbon future' developed in the preparatory stage. The interviews were conducted in such a way as to maintain the position of the researcher as 'objective participant'. The questions were designed to test and probe the propositions coming out of the preparatory research using neutral phrases and ensuring the questions were not leading. The pre-planned question was the starting point to probe for further insights and clarification to draw out a full and rich picture of the interviewee's views.

The interviewer aimed to be empathetic with the views of the interviewee. Where stakeholder views were challenged this was through presenting the proposition, not through confronting the views expressed. Each interview was therefore a meeting of minds even though the interviews took widely diverse directions. It was particularly interesting to discuss aviation from an industry perspective counterposed with the environmental view. In the former, a picture emerged of an industry with tight margins and under threat; in the latter, there was deep concern at the environmental impact and a belief that flying should be curtailed. Both positions were articulated well but the researcher could see and understand at first-hand the polarized nature of the debate.

Some interviewees started the interview with a very clear position. For example, one of the package holiday customers, knowing only the general theme of the research, started the interview with a robust defence of his 'right to fly' even before the interview started: 'unless you are going to tell me there is a new way ... I cannot see how we cannot burn the fuel. We will meet that expense one way or another in order to continue.' The interview evolved along the lines that flying 'is the most direct and economic way to get from A to B in a given timeframe'. He also explained that, 'Yes, I am very keen on the idea of protecting the environment but at the same time there is a cost to protect the environment.' This developed into a positive discussion around a new model of sustainable aviation. The interviewee came around to the view by the end of the interview: 'We might as well start with aviation because it is the one everyone sees, everyone uses, everyone is aware of.'

Most interviews were face to face and all were recorded and transcribed. This is important when the interviewer is taking a participatory role, as it is so easy to fall into the trap of thinking you have heard what you were hoping to hear as you seek to shape policy (Rubin & Rubin 2012). The transcribed interview does not lie. It also became clear on the first few interviews that the interviewer had, in small ways, compromised neutrality by offering a personal view. This was good in terms of building rapport but, it was decided, best avoided for subsequent interviews.

During the interview, the 'low-carbon future' was introduced after exploring issues around the current model. The interview was paused to introduce the model and the interviewee was allowed to ask informal questions to ensure they understood the model before the interview resumed. In a few cases the interview took place over Skype; in this case an e-mail to support the presentation of the new model was sent once the interview had commenced and the interviewee invited to open it at the appropriate stage of the interview to support the discussion.

Overall, data gathered through interviews within the structured framework was of good quality. Some of the most useful data came out of the additional probing and on-the-fly questions responding to the initial answer to the pre-planned question. This interview process could not have been contracted out to someone without deep engagement in the research or placed within a questionnaire. The engagement between the interviewer and interviewee was based upon capturing a deeply shared understanding of the particular stakeholder perspective.

4.10 Analysis

The first stage of the analysis of the empirical data was to cross-reference the responses from each interviewee with the propositions generated in Phase 1 of the research. These data were considered together to build a case about whether the proposition was supported, or not, and to draw out associated insights. This themed presentation of the data around the propositions became the prime way to access the data for the subsequent high-level analysis and drawing together of the overall findings.

Whilst sorting the data according to the structure established in the research protocol, the data was also examined for other emerging issues or themes that had not been anticipated. One of these was 'noise' which was not judged to be a major issue in this research because of the focus on the overall emissions from aviation. However, noise was found to be a very important consideration for politicians and the industry because of the vocal and effective opposition of residents near airports. The implication for this research was that where aircraft engine design involved trade-offs between noise and fuel efficiency, it could not be assumed that efficiency would win out. Another issue which was expected, but its importance had been missed in writing the research protocol, was the issue of carbon trading. The initial research had identified this but had concluded that although the industry talked about carbon trading, this appeared to be a public relations exercise and unlikely to act as the driver of significant change. However, it was found that reliance on carbon trading as the way forward for aviation was deep-rooted. There was a genuine belief that carbon trading would be the future, allowing aviation to continue on its present path with marginally higher costs through paying for reductions elsewhere in the global economy. This position was identified as likely to be one of the barriers to making real progress.

The output from the analytic stage, and foundation for the findings, was a full set of transcribed interviews together with the same data sorted by propositions arising from the analysis carried out at the preparatory phase. These well supported the extraction of the findings.

4.11 Findings

The first aim of the research was to identify a way forward for sustainability in aviation. It was known at the outset that this would entail challenging the stalemate in aviation policy and tackling the difficult task of reconciling economic objectives with environmental constraints. The deep analysis of Phase 1 defined the dynamics of the current industry and identified a possible way forward based on the insight that flying slower could be much more fuel-efficient. The analysis supported the notion of deploying a new breed of air vehicle to support a different economic model with an altered passenger experience. It was found that there was near total ignorance amongst all stakeholders that such a future could be possible. The stakeholder reaction was generally favourable, especially amongst environmentalists, one of whom said, 'I would be quite happy to change jobs and become part of the PR for this type of thing.' The aviation industry was the main sticking point; the belief was that the degree of change was more than the industry could handle. This concurred with the Phase 1 analysis which had shown that parts of the industry could face bankruptcy. One notable exception was an aviation company seeking to build and deploy a low-carbon air vehicle, which was finding it difficult to make headway. Interestingly, everyone in the industry, including this company, believed that the government was unlikely to make the policy changes required. For their part, government stakeholders could see the merits of the future proposed, and accept that in the end it could prevail, but it was felt that there were higher political priorities. It was noted also that the political cycle was a hindrance to the long-term policy thinking required. Although passengers were very resistant to the notion of restrictions on their ability to fly, there was near unanimous support for the idea of a different model where to travel cheaply you would have to accept travelling slower. Overall, the research identified that there is a viable sustainable future path for aviation, if the government were to engage with shaping policy and the aviation industry were to accept it. However, without a trigger to persuade the government and the aviation industry to invest time and money, the stalemate is likely to remain.

The second research aim was to discover insights into the challenge of implementing sustainable policy which might be applicable, not just in aviation, but also in other sectors and other areas of policy. The central finding is that applying sustainability concepts without a deep reappraisal of the whole system leads only to marginal change in individual elements. This is the approach applied to aviation up to now and has blocked progress. Deliberation of sustainable policy requires examination of the whole system in its entirety followed by consideration of systemic change. A further observation is that stakeholders will inevitably resist the idea of change if they perceive it as something that is being taken away from them. The way to overcome such resistance is to be able to justify the action and point to a vision which shows that the package of changes is for the better. Presented in this way, it is possible to include negative components such as restrictions. People can be persuaded to accept these if a big picture of improvement can be communicated.

4.12 Reflections on action research case study methodology

The action research case study has proved to be appropriate where the research parameters can be clearly defined, allowing a specific research protocol to be crafted. This is likely to be the case for specific management or governmental challenges with well-defined characteristics. In such cases, logical analysis can lead to a logical solution but the unknown is how to bring stakeholders along. Bringing in the philosophy of action research gives the case study transformational power, allowing the researcher to engage with stakeholders as an objective active participant. This involves listening, observing and also acting as a proponent of what the analysis shows to be the sensible and logical solution. However, an action research case study can only ever be a catalyst for change, steering stakeholders towards solutions; the researcher does not have the power to force adoption.

The action research case study is appropriate in situations where there is a stalemate despite the existence of a logical way forward. The carefully structured methodology presented here is thought not to be appropriate in fuzzy situations where the nature of the challenge is hard to define and a more exploratory approach is required.

4.13 Conclusions

The action research case study methodology has worked well in support of this investigation into the challenges of sustainability in the aviation industry. The apparent challenge under investigation was economic, technical and environmental, but the main barriers were found to be people's attitudes, and solutions revolve around what people will embrace. The simple prime conclusion is that active engagement with people can be the key to brokering solutions to economic and technical challenges.

Although the research has not led to immediate change in aviation policy, the action-orientated approach has brought greater focus, depth and insight. When the objective is to broker a solution the researcher has to confront and resolve dilemmas. With other research methodologies it may seem acceptable to record quandaries and note opposing views. The action-orientated research conveyed the strong intention to do more than observe and record, and thus delivered a stronger analysis and a more useful outcome than would be possible with the researcher as a neutral observer.

The 'action research case study' has the potential to tackle difficult issues and is not just the realm of academics. Management consultancy engages in activities that can look very much like action research. However, clients are often reluctant to pay for consultants to spend time on research, preferring resources to be applied promptly to analyse the problem and provide immediate recommendations for a solution (Frohan et al. 1976; Ormerod 1996). Academics may bend in the other direction, preferring to theorize rather than search for and drive through solutions. This author argues that the 'academic consultant' or 'consultant academic' is best placed to carry out effective action research, thus ensuring an effective balance between the research component (discovering causes and building hypotheses) and taking action (identifying changes likely to lead to improvements and setting them in train). Such research is an amalgam of academic analysis, consultancy and direct involvement. The challenge is to ensure the rigour expected by academia, to maintain the practicality of consultancy, and to channel the commitment to finding a solution which comes with personal engagement with the issues.

Beyond this research project and building on these findings, the author continues to engage with seeking to transform the aviation sector. For further research, it would be interesting to apply the methodology presented here to other sustainability challenges in other sectors, and explore whether the 'action research case study' has wider applicability and passes the tests of practice.

Note

1   This chapter was first published in the journal *Action Research* (McManners 2016a).

5 Sustainability in aviation

How concerns about carbon emissions will reshape the industry[1]

5.1 Introduction

Aviation is a global industry and integral component of the world economy, connecting people and places and facilitating trade. Sustainability in aviation is a difficult challenge with CO_2 emissions contributing to climate change. Meanwhile, as global aviation expands, there is widespread indifference to imposing restrictions on what is seen as a successful industry. There are opportunities for further growth, particularly in the large emerging economies of the Far East and India, where aviation has an important role (Bowen 2000; Hooper 2005; Evans 2014). The evident economic contribution of aviation as an enabler of international trade and tourism tends to overpower discussion of the environmental impact.

Aviation is responsible for 2–3 per cent of global emissions, and there are concerns that these emissions are at high altitude where their impact on the climate may be greater (Lee et al. 2010). The efficiency of the world's aircraft fleet has been improving at approximately 1.5 per cent annually (IATA 2014) as new aircraft are purchased and older aircraft retired. However, this reduction is eclipsed by the overall growth in capacity, such that emissions are on a steep upward trajectory. Currently, there are no firm plans to limit emissions, although there are proposals coming from the industry to include aviation in a global carbon market requiring airlines to offset their emissions or buy carbon credits.

There is a highly polarized debate about the future of aviation. On one side there are small groups of environmentalists in opposition. On the other, passengers and industry like affordable flights, and governments are reluctant to tackle an issue on which the public are not asking for change (Gössling & Peeters 2007; Lassen 2010). Aviation policy is stuck on its current course with little sign of any substantive change. Should aviation remain a special case for exemption from emission controls or is there a way to solve the dilemma between the benefits of aviation and its environmental impact?

The chapter starts with the historic context before outlining relevant aviation policy and the findings of the initial in-depth analysis. From this foundation, a vision of a possible future for aviation is developed and crafted into a proposed alternative model. The stakeholder reaction to this future model is reported, leading into a discussion about the way forward. Finally, there is a section on what might trigger such change in aviation before drawing the threads of the discussion together in the conclusions.

The analysis indicates that there is a potential way forward for aviation which reconciles economic and environmental objectives. This could lead to a bright future for aviation, but it will be different from now. A step change in aviation is required, which will be highly disruptive to the industry as it navigates the transition to a low-carbon model. Passengers will still be able to fly, but to fly fast will be expensive. It also became clear, through the course of the research, that the transformation will not commence until concern over the climate and public acceptance of the need for change push politicians to make the required alterations to policy.

5.2 Historic context

Developments in aviation, particularly step changes in technology, have historically come about through the application of technologies developed for the military. For example, the first Golden Age of aviation followed World War I, as aircraft developed for military needs were put to civilian use. The second Golden Age was after World War II, as the jet engine, developed in the later stages of the war in the search for greater speed for fighter aircraft, was deployed into the first generation of jet airliners. When there is a military need, arising from a national crisis, governments find the investment required.

Innovation today in the civil airline industry is not so much in aircraft design – although there is steady and gradual improvement of tried and tested models – but instead is focussed on business models. The low-cost aviation model has completely rewritten the commercial rules, making flying accessible to many more people and resulting in a huge expansion in the number and capacity of routes. From a passenger perspective, aviation has never been so good. Aircraft are fast and reliable, and tickets are affordable to a wide spread of society. There seems little sign of willingness to put this at risk to bring emissions under control.

It is suggested here that the next significant milestone in aviation history could be low-carbon flight. The motivating reason is growing concern over climate change and possible consequences (WEF 2013). If the impacts of climate change grow into a crisis, fuelling demands for emission reduction, this could signal the start of the Third Golden Age of aviation (McManners 2012) as policy shifts in support of a new generation of low-carbon air vehicles.

5.3 Aviation and climate policy

Policy for aviation and climate policy sit in different silos and are driven by different priorities. Aviation policy is focussed on growth and safety, whilst climate policy is focussed on bringing carbon dioxide emissions under control.

There is an inherent tension between, on the one hand, championing growth in a sector currently dependent on carbon-intensive technology and, on the other, holding emissions in check.

For aviation policy, the Convention on International Civil Aviation (ICAO 2006) is the overarching policy framework covering everything from airport design and safety procedures to security and rules about the application of custom duties. The aims and objectives are contained in Article 44 including the primary objective to 'ensure the safe and orderly growth of international civil aviation throughout the world'. There is no mention in the objectives of emissions or environmental impact; in fact, the words 'environment', 'carbon' or 'emissions' do not appear anywhere in the text.

Responsibility for climate policy rests with the United Nations Framework Convention on Climate Change (UNFCCC). The UNFCCC delegated the issue of allocation and control of emissions from aviation to the Subsidiary Body for Scientific and Technological Advice (SBSTA) (UNFCCC 1995). The SBTA considered the issue at their first meeting in 1995 and has kept it on the agenda with little substantive progress over the next 20 years except to invite the ICAO to work on the issue and report back (UNFCCC 2009; UNFCCC 2013). It may be pragmatic to delegate the development of policy for emissions from aviation to the ICAO, but as emissions reduction measures are a threat to continued growth, it is perhaps not surprising that progress moves at a glacial pace. The goals put forward by the ICAO are stated in its submission to the SBSTA (ICAO 2010a):

- global aspirational goal of 2 per cent annual fuel efficiency improvement up to year 2050;
- a medium-term global aspirational goal from 2020 that would ensure that while the international aviation sector continues to grow, its global CO_2 emissions would be stabilized at 2020 levels;
- development of a framework for market-based measures for carbon emissions.

More recent work by the ICAO (2013) has focussed on the development of sustainable biofuel for aviation under the rationale that overall net emissions would reduce and therefore have less climate impact.

On the face of it, there would appear to be progress in coordinating aviation and climate policy but on closer examination there are neither firm plans nor targets with any more substance than 'aspirational'. The reaction to these goals was explored in interviews with aviation stakeholders. Environmentalists were very sceptical, passengers did not understand or care very much, and even those inside the industry did not have a grasp of how these aspirations were to be achieved. In the industry there is hope that shifting to burning biofuel can be a large part of achieving the stated goals, but other experts interviewed as part of the research stated that the quantity of biofuel required was unrealistic.

The research examined whether a more realistic policy to limit emissions might be possible. This uncovered a key barrier to progress in Article 24 of the Convention on International Civil Aviation (ICAO 2006: 11):

> Aircraft on a flight to, from, or across the territory of another contracting State shall be admitted temporarily free of duty, subject to the customs regulations of the State. Fuel, lubricating oils, spare parts, regular equipment and aircraft stores on board an aircraft of a contracting State, on arrival in the territory of another contracting State and retained on board on leaving the territory of that State shall be exempt from customs duty, inspection fees or similar national or local duties and charges.

The consequence of Article 24 is that it prevents countries from taxing aviation fuel, because if a country cannot tax the fuel carried aboard an aircraft then any country leading with imposing a fuel tax would be at an economic disadvantage. The advice to airlines in textbooks of aviation economics is to fuel where prices are low and tanker fuel into higher-cost locations (Vasigh et al. 2008). A government stakeholder said about the UK possibly leading with taxing aviation fuel, 'If unilaterally the UK government decided then you wouldn't have so many people flying out of London. It wouldn't be used as a hub airport.' The UK is not going to take the risk that airlines shift their long-haul flights to other European airports. The governmental view is that if there is to be tax on aviation fuel it has to come about through international agreement and coordinated action. The problem is that aviation policy is not a priority. 'I don't think governments are not prepared to expend political capital, I just think there are so many other things on the agenda.' From a passenger perspective, most people were not aware that aviation fuel is free of tax, and all passenger stakeholders thought it should be taxed, with some wanting to see the tax used specifically to support the development of low-carbon aviation.

There was a range of views amongst the general business community about whether aviation fuel should be taxed. Within the aviation industry specifically, all stakeholders were confident that tax would not be imposed, and none of them had plans for this eventuality. The conclusion with regard to Article 24 is that whilst it remains in place, aviation fuel will remain free of tax and there is little commercial incentive to start planning the switch to low-carbon aviation.

Another major component of the current policy debate about climate and aviation policy is the potential of trading carbon. Interviews with aviation industry stakeholders made it clear that delivery of the industry's aspirational goals was dependent on the implementation of 'market-based measures'. Assuming that an effective global carbon market can be achieved – a big assumption – the outcome in real terms will be aviation continuing on much the same trajectory by buying carbon credits from the carbon market. The aviation industry finds this policy attractive because, apart from marginal cost increases, the overall commercial model is unchanged. Policy makers also seem to find it convenient to park the aviation emission problem at the doors of a carbon market without thinking through the long-term consequences. This research looked beyond the limitations of current policy to explore whether a more robust and realistic solution might be possible.

5.4 Initial in-depth analysis

An in-depth analysis was carried out focussed on the possibilities of transforming aviation, drawing on the literature, policy documents and other reports. This was carried out prior to embarking on the empirical research to tease out the logic of the situation before interviewing stakeholders. It was clear that the industry is highly regulated with substantial sunk costs and high inertia. By its nature aviation is resistant to change, but the initial analysis showed the need for change and strong grounds to challenge the status quo. This led to developing a set of assumptions about the future of aviation to frame the empirical research:

- The importance of climate change in world policy will grow and the urgency of taking action will increase.
- If the legacy of the current air transport system could be put aside, we would not now design a system based almost totally on fast-jet technology.
- Technology is advancing so rapidly that if we can identify a way forward within the parameters of sound science, engineers can design and build a solution.
- The key insight from science is that speed requires energy and high speed requires a lot of energy. The converse is that deciding on a slower design speed for an air vehicle will require significantly less energy to push it through the air.
- Fundamental to any future for aviation is safety.

These assumptions provide a basis for a model of a possible future for sustainable aviation.

5.5 A possible future for aviation

The ICAO concludes in its assessment of aircraft technology and the environmental impact (ICAO 2010b: 77):

> Currently, policy makers are experiencing pressure from society to find rapid measures to mitigate the impact of aviation on the environment, and particularly on climate change. Meanwhile, industry is constrained by having to operate within the unchanged rules of physics.

A fundamental rule of the physics of flight is that to fly requires energy and to fly fast requires a lot of energy. Currently the industry is locked into using fast jets which intrinsically burn a lot of fuel, and this mindset puts a limit on feasible emissions reduction. Breaking this mindset opens inquiry to other options and possible solutions based on different flight vehicles.

On 6 May 1937, the German passenger airship LZ 129 Hindenburg was engulfed in flames attempting to dock with the mooring mast on arrival at Air Station Lakehurst in the United States. It had taken off from Frankfurt, Germany, on the evening of 3 May and waited for bad weather to ease before making its final approach. Pictures of the airship rupturing and being destroyed in a fireball were captured by newsreel cameras and were shown around the world. In an industry where the perception of safety is vital to the confidence of passengers, this was a huge blow. These memorable iconic images have blighted the prospects for airships from that day to this. The gas used to provide lift for the Hindenburg was the highly flammable gas hydrogen. Modern airships use helium, an inert gas which is extremely safe, so there is no logical reason not to resume the development path of the airship. The case against airships can be overturned but there has been no point in doing so because jet airliners are safe, reliable and fast. It is hard to argue the case that jet airliners should be replaced with something slower which has a safety question mark deeply etched in people's subconscious. There is currently no incentive to pour investment and development effort into a new generation of modern airships.

Aviation could have developed along a number of different paths, with the actual path being a quirk of history. Not only was the airship killed off by the Hindenburg, but propeller-driven aircraft were also side-lined after World War II as the path of aviation was set firmly towards the jet age. In the postwar euphoria there was no question that the jet engine was the future. Little thought was given to the jet's increased thirst for fuel compared with propeller-driven aircraft. Fuel was cheap, flying was for a privileged few, and there was little appreciation of the consequences for the climate. Interestingly, it is only the most modern jets which surpass the fuel per passenger kilometre figures of the 1950s' propeller-driven airliners. When the industry quotes steady improvements in efficiency it is reported against the baseline of the early fuel-guzzling jets, not against what other technologies could have delivered. As aviation technology moves forward, it is getting harder to squeeze better efficiency figures out of fast-jet technology because it is inherently energy intensive. If it is decided that fuel efficiency (low carbon) is the prime design parameter, effort could be shifted into reopening other development paths, applying modern technology to catch up on half a century of lack of investment.

To build up the vision of future aviation presented here, let us start by considering why we fly and whether we need to fly at all. From the interviews, four primary reasons emerged as to why flying is important. First, flying is seen as a key enabler of globalization facilitating trade in high-value urgent and perishable goods, and allowing business people to meet and negotiate deals that increase cross-border business. However, the world is waking up to the systemic risks of economic globalization (Goldin & Mariathasan 2014). Analysis through the lens of sustainability is starting to point to different macro-policy priorities than simply expanding trade. The short supply chains intrinsic to sustainable manufacturing and the need to cure fossil-fuel dependency lead to an economic model less dependent on high-capacity international transportation. Defending the current model of aviation on the grounds that the economy requires it is looking less tenable as we look forward. It is not just that virtual reality conferencing technologies are making face-to-face meetings less necessary but the whole focus on global integration as the basis of macroeconomic policy should be questioned.

Second, aviation supports tourism, which is a major source of income, particularly for some of the poorest countries with little else to trade. However, tourism income is not dependent on flying fast. The empirical research showed that, although business people will continue to want to travel fast and are willing to pay to do so, people travelling for leisure were generally content with the idea of travelling slower provided the experience was better than the current cramped economy cabin.

The third reason people like to fly is to travel for work opportunities and leisure. However, people adopt commuter profiles that include flying, and travel more often for leisure, because it is increasingly affordable. These passengers are residents of rich countries or the rich elite of poor countries. There is no moral justification to make a special case for exemption from emission controls for these privileged people, but they will need to be offered a viable alternative to persuade them to support change.

A fourth reason that emerged from the interviews is the opinion that flying connects people and cultures, thus having the ability to diffuse tension and promote world peace. However, although this might be true, it makes no sense to use dirty technology to seek to cure one of the world's ills whilst causing another. To retain the benefits of flying, aviation should migrate to clean low-carbon technology.

5.6 Alternative model

The current passenger model of aviation is one that is familiar: First Class provides ample personal space and high-quality cabin service; Business Class provides good leg room and good food; Economy is cramped and the service basic. The underlying technology is the same; it is the space and level of service that varies. The insertion of new air vehicle technologies could completely change this model.

The aviation technology which will be deployed later this century is uncertain and will depend not only on developments in technology but also developments in economic and commercial models. One example with the potential to transform twenty-first century aviation is the hybrid air vehicle. This uses a combination of buoyancy and aerodynamic lift, looking like a hybrid between an aircraft and an airship. It has the potential to use much less energy, and for that energy to come from a wider range of sources. It has large spaces filled with helium to provide continual lift and a flattened aerodynamic shape which provides lift when it is propelled forward. The research found robust evidence that the design is sound in principle and a company that has the technology at prototype stage confirmed that it operates as expected. The barrier is that there is no commercial demand – outside some niche applications for heavy-lift capability into difficult-to-access locations. No one, including the small company designing them, is contemplating seriously that such air vehicles could replace jet aircraft. Modern jets are reliable and fast, and airports are designed to accommodate them. Fuel is cheap and its tax-free status means that the aviation industry is confident that it will remain cheap as they make future plans. There is no business case to pay for the upheaval that would ensue if hybrid air vehicles were to replace parts of the main aviation infrastructure. However, in this analysis it is possible to contemplate, in concept, how aviation might look if hybrid air vehicles are introduced with the aim of achieving significant advances in overall fuel efficiency. See Figure 5.1.

This new model for aviation would have additional passenger service offerings hosted on hybrid air vehicles which, as well as being more efficient, will be slower: perhaps half the speed of current jet aircraft. Aviation experts pointed out that these large, relatively slow air vehicles would be affected more by weather conditions such as head winds making scheduling less certain. These disadvantages can be offset to an extent by the nature of the passenger experience. First Class on a hybrid air vehicle could be a luxurious experience, which could include a personal cabin. Business Class could include working facilities as good as many offices. Economy could include a couchette with ample leg room. For everyone, there could be space to move around and for entertainment like a compact cruise ship of the skies.

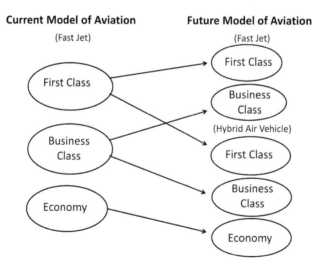

Figure 5.1 A low-carbon model for aviation

The situation with freight is that hybrid air vehicles could take a good chunk of the business from fast jets. The advantage of hybrid air vehicles is good lift capacity; the disadvantage is that delivery would be slower. High-value urgent deliveries would still go by fast jet but a lot of airfreight is less time-critical; a ship might be too slow, but doubling the delivery time compared with fast jet may have little impact. One stakeholder working in a small global business commented with regard to responding to the introduction of the new model of aviation:

> We might consider taking on new warehouses in different places trying to change the whole logistics network. A small business like us would take/ want at least a year and probably 18 months. I could imagine if we were three or four times the size that 18 months could be three years.

Considering such a revolution in aviation opens up a new frontier in aerospace to design and build low-carbon air vehicles. It may be possible to cover the upper surface of these large air vehicles with photovoltaic cells to gather energy from the sunlight which is much more reliable above cloud level. These could be used to power propellers driven by electric motors supplemented by other power sources such hydrogen fuel cells, although the Hindenburg legacy might delay the implementation of such ideas. Once the aero engineers are given the brief to design a relatively slow, highly efficient air vehicle that combines both buoyancy and aerodynamic lift, they might surprise us with the specific solution they offer. The current sticking point is that no one with substantial money to invest is asking the question and giving the engineers such a brief.

None of this is going to come about whilst policy protects fuel free of tax. To promote the new model, fuel will need to be more expensive by design, whether that is through taxation of fuel or taxation of carbon. This will mean that fast jets become relatively much more expensive. For affluent people in a hurry there will still be First Class and Business Class, with little change except for the greater expense. Economy Class on jets will effectively cease to exist in that all seats on jets will be more expensive. Passengers on a tight budget would only have the hybrid service available to them. Whether such restrictions could be acceptable to passengers was one of the main aims of the empirical research as reactions to the model were explored with stakeholders.

5.7 Stakeholder consultation

The empirical phase of the research focussed on five main stakeholder groups: 'aviation industry', 'environmentalists', 'other industry', 'governmental', 'passengers' and the sub-group 'package holiday passengers'. The aim was to engage with stakeholders to fully understand their position, probing, testing and at times challenging their view. The research methodology combined the ethos of action research with Robert Yin's approach to case study research (Yin 2014). The process was structured, recorded and documented to ensure the research was both impartial and rigorous despite the direct engagement of the researcher with the issues. The key specific insights into stakeholder attitudes are summarized below in four categories: current attitudes; reaction to the proposed future model; reasons for the policy stalemate; and ideas about a way forward.

5.7.1 Current attitudes

Stakeholder attitudes to the current model of aviation are highly polarized. On one side, passengers like affordable flights and are resistant to the notion of restrictions; on the other, environmentalists think that flying should be curtailed. The attitude of aviation industry stakeholders is conservative, reflecting a highly regulated industry. They expect aviation to continue to grow based on current airport and aircraft design parameters. People in the industry are also confident that the government will not change policy with respect to tax on aviation fuel. This view is supported by governmental stakeholders who see no reason to tackle such a difficult issue when there is no popular demand for change.

5.7.2 Reaction to the proposed future model

Both environmentalists and passengers were supportive of the new model for aviation when it was explained to them. An environmentalist and leading campaigner against the expansion of aviation said in response to the new model:

> I am not against flying as such. No. I would say against the current model of aviation. I would be quite happy to change jobs and become part of the PR for this type of thing.

People in the aviation industry took a different view and were concerned at the impact on their business and the disruption of implementing the new model. Governmental stakeholders could see the theoretical merits but were concerned at the possible economic consequences and worried about the passenger response. Industry stakeholders outside aviation assumed that if it happened, they would have to embrace it, and focussed on thinking through how they would respond.

5.7.3 Reasons for the policy stalemate

There was broad agreement that there is a stalemate in policy. The discussions with stakeholders exposed a range of views which seemed to hinge in different ways on the issue of tax-free fuel. Environmentalists expressed anger that fuel is not taxed. Passengers also thought it was wrong that airlines did not pay tax on fuel and right that policy should change so that aviation fuel would be taxed in the future. The industry did not believe that the status quo would change.

Governmental stakeholders did not believe it was in their power to change international policy to allow taxation of fuel. Most stakeholders acknowledged that the case for low-carbon aviation is stalled whilst cheap fuel is available without restriction.

5.7.4 Ideas about a way forward

In discussing the way forward, passengers and environmentalists agreed that attitudes to climate change would have to harden to provide the context in which a debate over radical change in aviation could be taken seriously. All stakeholders doubted that the aviation industry could lead, with a number suggesting that there would have to be government support to develop the required technology.

5.8 Leveraging the vision of sustainable aviation

The dilemma with aviation is that we want to be able to fly, but flying burns a lot of fuel. It would seem that if we want to fly, we have to burn the fuel. Failure to address this dilemma means the argument revolves around flying or not flying. The purpose of presenting a vision of the future is to break this circular argument.

First, it is interesting to examine the aviation industry's vision of a sustainable future. Their solution is to replace conventional aviation fuel with biofuel. This would require a massive expansion of biofuel production. To be sustainable, this would need to be produced without displacing food crops from agricultural land or deforestation to bring new land into biofuel feedstock production. Leaving aside the relatively small quantities of biofuel which could be produced from organic waste, the sustainable biofuel would have to come from advanced biofuel production methods. An example is transparent water tanks containing algae which use sunshine to produce a feedstock which can be converted to biofuel. These could be located in desert regions – where the world has no shortage of space – but such biofuel will be expensive. This is not just in terms of cost but also in terms of the resources required to build and operate the production facilities. If we think through this vision of the future for aviation, we can conclude that sustainable aviation biofuel will be expensive. To prepare aviation for such a future, and set the foundation for sustainable biofuel production, the economic lever required is to ramp up the cost of conventional aviation fuel. However, to do this now would be politically difficult because flying would become significantly more expensive, making it the preserve of the wealthy. The aviation industry is aware that this is the case and finds it convenient that their vision means no change to the status quo anytime soon.

Second, let us examine the vision presented here of a slower design speed for a new breed of air vehicle which is more fuel efficient. It may be able to cruise above cloud height using solar power from panels on its large upper surface driving electric motors. It would need another fuel source to take off and when pushing into a head wind, but overall it would need much less fuel than a fast jet. If we think through this vision of the future, to make it viable requires developing the technology of relatively slow efficient flight. To prepare aviation for such a future, the economic lever required is to ramp up the cost of conventional aviation fuel to make the hybrid design a commercial prospect. With this vision, the main political difficulty has been side-stepped. This research found that flying slower if you are on a budget is acceptable when the rich are paying for the privilege of flying fast. Flying would still be available to all those who fly now, but flying fast would incur a significant premium. Passengers can be persuaded to accept such a vision, and if it is acceptable to the electorate it becomes possible for government to act, but the main aviation industry players will not be supporting this vision. To accept the vision of low-carbon aviation is to initiate a disruptive transformation in which there will be corporate casualties. This is where capitalism is very good at orchestrating the required creative destruction but this has to be initiated by forces outside the industry.

The reality is likely to draw on both visions, with a slower hybrid air vehicle taking a significant proportion of traffic and a smaller premium fast-jet market fuelled by sustainable biofuel. It is interesting to note that the action required is the same for both visions. The required action is to ramp up the cost of conventional aviation fuel by changing the rules of international aviation to allow (and even encourage) the taxation of fuel. If we pause to reflect, it doesn't really matter which vision is closer to reality provided it serves the political purpose of securing agreement to tax aviation fuel. In this regard, the hybrid air vehicle model is a much easier sell, so it makes sense to play down possible difficulties and push ahead with support for the technology so that the vision is credible and believable. I believe that it is a credible future model but I understand why the current industry will do all in its power to oppose it. People outside the industry who allow discussion to focus on the possible limitations of low-carbon aviation need to understand that this may block progress by closing the door of political acceptability just as a way has been identified to open it.

5.9 A way forward

Drawing together the strands of the investigation, a possible way forward could be identified. The two key players are the government and the aviation industry. The former has responsibility for aviation policy and the latter has the most to lose from a botched transition. The current situation is that government does not want to expend political capital on changing aviation policy and the industry is focussed on defending the status quo. For this to change, government will have to start thinking creatively beyond the confines of the electoral cycle; and industry be persuaded to invest for a time horizon beyond a short-term financial return.

There is a precedent which gives confidence that this might be possible. In the 1970s, the Danish government decided to capitalize on its abundant wind power potential by supporting the development of wind turbine technology (Lewis & Wiser 2007). This was many years before demand for wind power took off. Some forward-looking parts of Danish industry rose to the challenge and, with government support, invested time and resources. Denmark is now leading the world in wind turbine technology. A country could take a similar strategic approach with the design and production of hybrid air vehicles, to become, in due course, world leader in the new model of twenty-first century aviation.

Three activities are proposed for governments to consider taking an instrumental role in nudging aviation towards a sustainable future:

- The technology of hybrid air vehicles should be considered for government support such as tax breaks, subsidies and research grants.
- Set up a team within government with the remit to work towards amending the International Convention on Civil Aviation, in particular to altering Article 24 with a view to supporting and even promoting taxation of aviation fuel.
- Consider a public information programme to educate people of a vision of sustainable aviation to start to build public support for policy change.

All three activities could run in parallel towards a point when the technology of hybrid air vehicles is proven; the public accept the idea; and international diplomacy moves in favour of changing the Convention on Civil Aviation.

5.10 Triggering change

Currently there is little appetite to break the stalemate in aviation policy. There are no obvious winners in leading a transformation in aviation, except perhaps the global atmosphere represented by environmentalists, but their power is weak. The best chance of significant change is that one or more countries decide that there is long-term strategic advantage for their aerospace sector through supporting such a transformation. Having supported their industry to be ready to reap the rewards, they might then use growing concern at climate change to push for policy change in the international arena. The reason would be to reduce emissions from aviation to reduce the impact on the environment; the incentive would be to be at the forefront of a huge global market in hybrid air vehicles.

5.11 Conclusion

The research entered a highly polarized debate about the future of aviation with the high-level research question: 'Should aviation remain a special case for exemption from emission controls or is there a way to solve the dilemma between the benefits of aviation and its environmental impact?' The answers emerged that 'no' there is no valid justification for exemption and 'yes' there is a way to solve the dilemma. There will have to be change, and the sustainability perspective points towards starting the transformation sooner rather than later. However, it was found that no stakeholder has a direct interest in campaigning for change, except perhaps environmentalists, but their voice is marginalized and they have chosen to focus on opposition rather than making the positive case for change.

Aviation remains stuck on its current path because of inertia consisting of a number of factors. First, unwieldy international regulations; second, the industry has substantial investment in the existing fleets and ground infrastructure; third, passengers are content with the current model; finally, safety is critical to making the industry risk averse, particularly with regard to a new generation of passenger airships where the Hindenburg legacy continues to cast a long shadow.

The research identified a solution that benefits all stakeholders in the longer term but people are blinkered by the short term. This is not surprising because there will be short-term pain for the aviation industry and restrictions for passengers as well as the need for effort and engagement from government. The vision for aviation outlined here provides both an improved passenger experience and makes emission control feasible. As concern over climate change grows, pressure for action will increase, but this alone is unlikely to be enough to break the policy stalemate. This research indicates that promulgation of a vision of better aviation will be prerequisite to garnering public support for the required changes in policy. The policy lessons for how to incorporate sustainability into policy are the subject of the next chapter.

Note

1   This chapter was presented at the 5th World Sustainability Forum, 7–9 September 2015, Basel, Switzerland.

6 Developing policy integrating sustainability

A case study into aviation[1]

6.1 Introduction

There is growing support for the concept of sustainability but there is a large divergence between rhetoric (policy) and reality (practice) (Barr 2012). This is understandable because deep analysis to find a true balance between economic, social and environmental factors is difficult. The aviation sector was selected for a case study to examine the process of developing sustainable policy because it stands out as the most difficult sector to implement sustainability (Nijkamp 1999; Gössling & Upham 2009; Daley 2010; Watson 2014). The UK was chosen for practical reasons and because there is a history of attempts to apply sustainability to aviation. The UK Sustainable Development Commission (SDC) which operated between 2000–2011 carried out an investigation into aviation (SDC 2008a). Meetings were convened and focus groups consulted, but the results did not go much beyond clarifying that stakeholder views were highly polarized and that further investigation was needed (SDC 2008b). The difficulty of the challenge in aviation, which made it so hard for the SDC to have an impact, makes it ideal for an examination of barriers to sustainability and exploration of how they might be overcome. If progress could be made in this most intractable area of policy then lessons might be learnt applicable to other sectors to mainstream sustainability in policy formulation.

The challenge of sustainability is universal, requiring transdisciplinary research, with the social sciences having an important role in framing such societal challenges (Diedrich et al. 2011). The particular research reported here was part of an investigation at the interface between socio-economic and environmental policy, drawing on perspectives from geography, economics, engineering and business. The research had two stages; an investigative stage followed by an empirical stage comprising 28 stakeholder interviews. The aim of the case study was to investigate a sustainable way forward for aviation. The aim of this chapter is to tease out general lessons arising from the case study for how sustainability can be incorporated into high-level policy formulation.

The first part of the chapter sets the scene with sections on background to the research and an outline of the methodology. There follows a summary of key findings from the in-depth sustainability analysis and the stakeholder consultation. The second half of the chapter focusses on the insights that the research provides for the process of facilitating the formulation of sustainable policy. These are discussed under the primary themes which emerged from the research: 'long-term strategic planning'; 'facilitation of dialogue between stakeholders'; 'government support for innovation'; and 'educating the public'.

6.2 Background

Global aviation is on a steep growth path driven by the low-cost business model and rapid expansion in the Far East, India and other emerging markets (Bowen 2000; Hooper 2005; Evans 2014). Despite steady improvements in aircraft efficiency CO_2 emissions are rising in step with this growth and are currently 2–3 per cent of global CO_2 emissions (Owen et al. 2010). Although measures to limit emissions are under discussion, led by the International Civil Aviation Organization (ICAO), there are no firm plans to control emissions and, due to concerns about the economic consequences, there is little appetite to do so. Aviation is a key enabler of the global economy, connecting markets and facilitating international trade (Grubesic & Matisziw 2012). It also underpins tourism, which is a significant source of revenue for many countries (Perovic 2013).

Aviation is a prime example of a direct clash between environmental and economic policy and so a good test-bed to explore how to strike an appropriate balance. When policy makers focus on economic outcomes, it can mean that the economic case comes first, with environmental factors relegated to an impact assessment. Such an environmental impact assessment might lead to adjustment of some aspects but it tends to come too late in the process to rethink the fundamental basis of the proposal. Introducing the concept of sustainability into policy formulation has the potential to bring a more complete perspective to bear on the options to be considered. In aviation, the dilemma between continuing to reap the economic benefits whilst bringing the environmental impact within safe bounds is particularly difficult (Walker & Cook 2009). As with many attempts to drive forward the sustainability agenda, a narrow economic view tends to dominate the mainstream debate (Hopwood et al. 2005). An alternate approach, applied in the research reported here, is to bring sustainability to the fore. Instead of seeking to make the most economic case sustainable, this is reversed to making the most sustainable solution economically viable (McManners 2014). In aviation this is a major shift in mindset. Currently the question is phrased as: this is aviation as we know it, so how do we mitigate the emissions? This leads to consideration of marginal changes to reduce the emissions of each element of the current system. Here a different question has been posed: what would a low-carbon air transport system look like? The definition of low-carbon air transport used here is aviation that is not reliant on fossil fuel over the long term, coupled with a transition path that matches the decarbonization timescale recommended by the scientists of the United Nations Framework Convention on Climate

Change (UNFCCC). This is necessarily imprecise because, currently, the UNFCCC has no agreed limits on aviation emissions. It should be noted that there is much discussion within the aviation industry that growth in the current model of air transportation can continue provided the fuel is sustainable biofuel. This is justified on the basis that the carbon emitted is not fossil carbon. The research found this claim to be disingenuous because the amount of biofuel required is unrealistic and in any case there will be multiple other demands on limited supplies. Whatever the fuel source, a sustainable future for aviation will have to shift from high to low carbon.

6.3 Overview of research methodology

The methodology employed was a novel approach developed for the research, which is described in detail in a recent paper in the journal *Action Research* (McManners 2016a) and reproduced in Chapter 4. This 'action research case study' combined the orientation to inquiry offered by action research (Bradbury 2013) with the case study methodology of Robert Yin (Yin 2014). This allowed the researcher to go beyond the role of neutral observer to take on a participatory role whilst retaining academic rigour. The research had two stages, starting with an investigative stage using a range of sources, which included policy documents and reports of previous studies. The objective of this phase was to understand the current situation with regard to aviation policy in some depth in order to be able to develop a theoretical viable sustainable future without the analysis being constrained by vested interests or established existing policy assumptions.

The second stage of the research was a series of 28 interviews to add depth to the analysis and test this vision of a possible future with stakeholders. The interviews were interactive engagements based on a series of propositions to be tested, including alternative propositions for which there was no evidence in order to test the process. Interviewees were selected to achieve a spread across stakeholder groups to capture the viewpoint of key interested parties (with some interviewees being members of more than one stakeholder group). The initial list of stakeholder groups was 'aviation industry', 'environmentalists', 'passengers', 'governmental' and 'industry outside aviation'. This was supplemented by a further sub-group of 'package holiday passengers' in response to the insight emerging from the research that less wealthy passengers could be the focus of resistance. This stakeholder group was used to explore what would be required to counter the perception of unfairness to such people arising from restrictions to aviation. The second-stage research was used to clarify the findings of the first stage and test reaction to the proposed alternative model for aviation.

6.4 In-depth sustainability analysis

The first stage of the research identified a viable sustainable future which is technically feasible and could be commercially viable. This built on previous analysis (McManners 2012) brought up to date with the latest developments in the aviation industry and the supporting technology. This is not a prediction of the future, but an example of one possible future model of aviation with low environmental impact. Currently aviation utilizes fast jets as the workhorse of the sky, with passenger segments defined by levels of service using the same underlying flying technology. People are familiar with their options to fly: First Class, Business Class or Economy. The problem with the industry, from a sustainability perspective, is that jet aircraft are inherently energy-intensive machines. The research identified that a step change in technology to slower more efficient air vehicles is likely to be the key to a sustainable future. There would still be a premium market for fast-jet travel but the mass market could shift to a new flying air vehicle. Such an air vehicle is likely to be a hybrid between an airship and an aircraft. The design parameters of hybrid air vehicles are being developed (Khoury 2012; Ceruti & Marzocca 2014), but they are not currently commercially viable except for niche applications as confirmed in the empirical research in an interview with a senior executive involved in developing the technology. The barrier to their development is that the international agreements which govern aviation mean that aviation fuel for international flights is tax free. There is no commercial incentive to tackle the difficult task of persuading people to accept slower travel when cost savings from the lower fuel burn are moderate. Fuel is a significant cost to airlines because they burn so much, but whilst it is tax free it is cheaper to stick with conventional jet aircraft. They are reliable and fast, which are the perfect attributes of an air transport system. The sustainable solution requires that international agreements are amended to allow (and perhaps require) the taxation of aviation fuel, or an equivalent measure such as a carbon tax. Fast jet transportation would become relatively more expensive supporting the business case for slower, more efficient air vehicles.

This model demonstrates that there is potentially a bright future for aviation, and highlights the important insight that a sustainable economic model is significantly different from the current model. In the model First Class and Business Class would still be hosted on jet aircraft for time-poor people who could afford the high prices. There would also be new passenger segments hosted on hybrid air vehicles. As they are a cross between an aircraft and airship, the requirement for space for helium to provide buoyancy means that these air vehicles would be large and spacious. The journey would be slower but hybrid air vehicles can host a better passenger experience. First Class could translate into a private cabin; Business Class could have facilities as good as most offices; and for Economy there would at least be good leg room and reclining couchettes. In effect, there would no longer be an Economy Class on fast jets, with people on a tight budget steered towards using a hybrid air vehicle service.

This positive vision of a sustainable future for aviation was instrumental in shifting the stakeholder consultation from an argument for and against the expansion of aviation to a discussion about the nature and form of low-carbon aviation. Note that the discussion was grounded in what is currently known to be possible without going into more speculative opportunities for further improvements. One such example is that large, relatively slow air vehicles, flying above cloud height, would be very good candidates for using electric engines running on solar power as part of the thrust package.

6.5 Stakeholder Consultation

The stakeholder consultation found that there is a growing realization within the aviation industry that sustainability matters, something an aviation stakeholder described as:

> Sustainability is about maintaining your licence to operate and securing your licence to grow, and if you don't get it right you don't get either. It is also about cost saving opportunities. So you get smarter about saving energy or saving fuel you don't just save CO_2 but a lot of money.

However, aviation industry stakeholders were not considering radical change in order to deliver a sustainable future; such thinking was not even on the radar. There was a solid belief that governments would not change policy and aviation fuel would remain free of tax. Business strategy was therefore based on a continuation of the current model of aviation. Nevertheless, the industry is responding to growing pressure to reduce emissions by putting forward aspirational targets to limit net emissions. The aviation industry proposes two ways to do this: first, by switching to sustainable biofuel, as this would be less carbon-intensive than kerosene. The UK aviation industry is putting lobbying effort behind this proposal (Sustainable Aviation 2014). However, an expert in the potential of biofuel described the aviation industry targets as, 'totally unrealistic'. The second aviation industry response to pressure for emissions reduction is the proposed introduction of market-based measures for trading carbon emissions from aviation (ICAO 2010a). Four out of five aviation industry stakeholders were convinced that this should be the way forward, although the details of the proposal have yet to be worked out.

All governmental stakeholders acknowledged the difficulty of the challenge: 'What tends to drive governments is short-term economics more so than long-term strategic planning. That is a challenge for a sector like aviation.' The research found no evidence that government was seriously engaging with long-term strategic planning in aviation and only one governmental stakeholder expressed a view that challenged the status quo. In line with the industry view, government supported a market-based approach, in conjunction with the use of sustainable alternative fuels, technological improvements to aircraft and operational improvements in air traffic management.

As for the taxation of aviation fuel, it was acknowledged that to tax aviation fuel would require international agreement, but a senior government stakeholder said:

My concern is that you will end up the country that leads the way suffering and I cannot see how we persuade the Chinese, the Indians and others to tax aviation fuel. I think for Europe and the States to go that way would be economic madness.

Both the UK aviation industry and government agreed that if the UK were to decide unilaterally to tax aviation fuel, Heathrow would become a short-haul regional airport, with other European airports acting as global hubs. A government official explained that within government circles, it was accepted that it would not be possible to renegotiate the Convention on International Civil Aviation (also known as the Chicago Convention), which prohibits the taxation of aviation fuel for international flights. The politician interviewed supported this view, suggesting that there were higher priorities: 'I don't think governments are prepared to expend political capital; there are so many other things on the agenda.'

Passengers were initially defensive of any notion that their ability to fly might be restricted, but when the alternative model was explained to them, just one passenger was in opposition due to his particular fear of flying and not wanting to spend longer in the air than absolutely necessary. On the one hand, business people, travelling on business, would still want to use the fast-jet service and assumed that their company would pay the extra cost. On the other, ten of the 11 passengers interviewed were content to trade time for money for leisure travel, particularly if it was a better travel experience. Environmentalists were keen to support the alternative model, with one leading campaigner against expansion at Heathrow commenting, 'I am not against flying as such. No. I would say against the current model of aviation. I would be quite happy to change jobs and become part of the PR for this type of thing.'

The overall finding was that a sustainable future for aviation was judged by almost all stakeholders to be desirable in principle, but the two main actors, government and the aviation industry, did not yet see a need or an incentive to act. The aviation industry is locked into a policy stalemate with aviation fuel free of tax; passengers are content with what is provided; and government is under little pressure to consider investing political capital in brokering change to international aviation agreements.

The research indicated a possible way forward for aviation policy but also clearly defined the current stalemate through different stakeholder perspectives. The rest of this chapter considers the elements of the possible way forward to break the stalemate in aviation policy and draw out generic lessons for bringing sustainability to bear on policy. These elements are the primary themes arising from the research data: first, the need for long-term strategic thinking and planning; second, the benefits of facilitating a dialogue between stakeholders; third, the useful role of government to support innovation in both technology and business models; fourth, the vital activity of educating the general public to generate support for necessary change.

6.6 Long-term strategic planning

Sustainability is about long-term balanced policy so it is fundamental that the thinking used to formulate such policy must be strategic and long term. Real-world policy will always come up against short-term challenges and resistance from vested interests, but the core analysis has to rise above these. The logic of the analysis has been followed through without such impediments to what would appear to be a sustainable solution. The first generic lesson from the research is the need to find space to think freely without hindrance. The barriers to avoid are not just those erected by people and organizations with a stake in the existing state of affairs, but also less obvious obstacles that arise due to a mindset based on intimate familiarity with the current system.

The particular barrier to long-term sustainable strategic thinking identified in the case study was the electoral cycle. This was highlighted by the topical issue of airport capacity in the South East of England with a Member of Parliament commenting:

> This goes back to the balance of sustainability and economic growth. We have an airports commission due to report back in July next year. I would love for whoever happens to be in government to actually for once follow through and actually go with the recommendations.

The decision over airport capacity is delayed because there is no agreed long-term sustainable strategy for aviation. The length of a typical political term is four or five years which is short-term in the context of planning for sustainability. Therefore a way is required to distance the high-level strategic policy from the political process. In a democracy, the elected politicians have to be persuaded of the value of cross-party cooperation and the delegation of strategic thinking to civil servants or appointed experts authorized to lead with formulation of sustainable policy. This would not eliminate short-term political influence but it would mean that the starting point for any policy could have taken sustainability fully on board. Subsequent political dealing may undermine long-term sustainability but starting the process with sustainable options would be a huge improvement compared with policy designed to suit short-term challenges with elements of sustainability tagged on. Politicians may not have the popular mandate to think strategically but having a strategic framework that survives beyond the term of a single administration is how to overcome this weakness of the democratic process.

The primary deduction, with respect to the process of formulating sustainable policy, is to carve out a space, in intellectual and practical terms, to think strategically and long term. This could be through a management team or appointed person charged with strategic sustainability, given the authority and resources to put forward an overarching framework within which the negotiation of particular policy takes place. The experiment in the UK with the SDC as an organization outside government, designed to hold the government to account, did not survive and has been disbanded. It might be better to earmark resources inside government to have direct power and influence. Instead of perpetuating the separation between mainstream policy and sustainability, it is suggested that the aim should be to fuse them into a single mindset, leading to policy that is sustainable by design.

6.7 Facilitation of dialogue between stakeholders

This case study into aviation showed how polarized views can be a barrier to seeking out solutions. It also showed that facilitation of dialogue between stakeholders can be useful in finding a way past such barriers. This concurred with feedback reported by the SDC on their aviation consultation process (SDC 2008c). At one extreme of the debate, the environmentalist view was that growth in aviation should be resisted and people should be persuaded to fly less: 'I think the public good would be served by curtailing the availability of all flights, affordable and expensive.' To this environmentalist, it was a black-and-white issue of for or against flying. On the other side of the debate, the aviation industry's view was summed up by a response to the possibility that aviation fuel might be taxed to provide the commercial incentive for low-carbon aviation. This director of one of Europe's airlines was concerned that it would have:

> Very dramatic effects on the aviation business today. It would cause catastrophic job losses not just in aviation but in all the industries that depend, directly and indirectly, on aviation. It would dramatically affect the costs of doing business and international trade. You would need to approach this very carefully.

To this senior business stakeholder, anything that might interrupt growth in aviation is to be resisted. The ruling logic in the aviation industry is that the industry needs continued growth and this will require increased emissions, so increased emissions are inevitable. This logic leads to the aviation industry favouring market mechanisms which allow airlines to pay for compensating reductions elsewhere in the economy. At each end of the debate, stakeholders held views that were logical within their own frame of reference, but the result was stalemate.

If stakeholders were to engage, share and challenge each other's views, without preconditions, it might become possible to have a useful dialogue. At the core of the environmentalists' demand is reduction in emissions. At the core of the industry demands is to be allowed to continue flying. From this foundation it becomes possible to note that the fast jet is not a fixed parameter but that there are other options. Once people's minds are opened to a possible future that all stakeholders might embrace, the discussion shifts from a confrontational debate to a shared discussion on how to handle the transition. In aviation there is such a chasm between the factions that there will need to be greater pressure, and more neutral arbitration along the lines of this research before such a positive dialogue can get established.

This research consisted of one-on-one discussion engaging positively with all those interviewed to facilitate an analysis which sidesteps a confrontation between environmentalists and the industry. Where a win–win solution can be identified, it has every chance of gaining support and being adopted. Where the sustainable solution is a win–lose of lose–win situation – as it is with aviation – it is more difficult. The future proposed for aviation was found to be beneficial to society and acceptable to passengers. Therefore it can be envisaged that the public should demand it and government should respond by changing policy. However, the current aviation industry has considerable investment in current fleets and ground infrastructure, much of which would become obsolescent. The aviation industry is not going to volunteer for a future which might bankrupt some of the main players. One of the aviation industry research participants withdrew when they saw the direction the research was taking. Although research ethics required that this data was removed from the analysis, the limited conclusion can be drawn that parts of the industry are very sensitive about entering into a dialogue where society could choose to impose a sustainable future on the industry.

It is suggested by this research that, in the general case, a group of stakeholders should be convened with a range of expertise and perspectives, and a way found to put aside organizational loyalties. There has been success with using stakeholder dialogue to drive sustainable innovation at the company level such as the case studies in Spain reported by Ayuso et al. (2006). At industry level, in difficult cases like aviation, it might require a facilitator to work with parties separately, as if arbitrating in a dispute, to lay the groundwork. In this group, separately or together, the consequences of sustainability can be considered to incubate ideas and test in theory what might be possible.

6.8 Government support for innovation

Aviation is a high-technology industry with substantial research and developments costs. It is estimated that Boeing invested $21 billion to develop its new flagship model the 787 Dreamliner (Schwartz & Busby 2014). Low-carbon air vehicles may eventually require similar levels of investment, although proof of concept would need much smaller amounts. A director of a company working on designs for hybrid air vehicles, interviewed for the research, estimated that circa £20 million would be sufficient to demonstrate that such designs are sound. The industry does not see a commercial case to invest, and until hybrid air vehicles exist, the general public do not see at first-hand a viable alternative to the fast jet. Until the public accept the idea of a different model, governments are not going to expend political capital to change international regulations for aviation. Until the regulations are changed to allow taxation of aviation fuel, the industry does not have a commercial basis to develop hybrid air vehicles. This is where the strategic role of government is required to break this vicious circle and support the development of the technology through its early stages.

Advances in civil aviation technology have often come about as spinoffs from technology developed for the military. The prime example is the jet engine developed towards the end of World War II in the search for greater speed for fighter aircraft. After the war this was the technology that ushered in the jet age, without worrying that jets were much thirstier than the propeller-driven airliners they replaced. Flying was for a privileged few, fuel was cheap and the climate consequences were not understood. With the huge expansion of aviation, and knowledge of the impact of emissions, the world of aviation needs to move beyond the jet age to the low-carbon age of flight with dramatically less environmental impact, but society cannot rely on defence budgets to pay for the development effort.

The sustainable model of aviation, developed within this research project, requires a significantly more efficient air vehicle, accepting that its greater efficiency will come from slower speed. A strategic defence study for the United States Congressional Budget Office assessed the technology of hybrid air vehicles to be viable using conventional turbo-prop engines (CBO 2005). However, the report noted that flying relatively slowly and relatively low made them vulnerable to enemy action, so did not recommend them for defence purposes. Major advances in aviation are often spinoffs from defence development. If defence is not going to fund the development of hybrid air vehicles, it will require investment from other sources, particularly in the development of low-carbon propulsion systems. When hybrid air vehicles finally exist, and have established a safe track record, and people become familiar with the concept, it should become easier to 'sell' a different model of aviation. If a country with a significant aerospace sector, like the UK, were to see this as part of the future model for aviation, a strategic decision could be taken to support UK industry in developing the technology. This would have parallels with Denmark's decision in the early 1990s to encourage and support Danish industry to develop wind turbines (Lewis & Wiser 2007). This was at a time when wind power was not in vogue but this far-sighted industrial policy means that Denmark is now home to a world-leading wind turbine industry. Low-carbon aviation is not now in vogue but facilitating early investment could have significant benefits as the era of low-carbon aviation dawns.

The general insight is that innovation in support of long-term strategic sustainability is hard for industry when the return is long term and the parameters are uncertain. Government has a valuable role to play, including direct financial support such as research grants and tax breaks. Government support could be as simple as removing uncertainty through policy to set a framework within which innovators and entrepreneurs have a reason to search for solutions. Formulating such policy needs the long-term strategic thinking which is fundamental to sustainability.

6.9 Educating the public

Public support will be vital to a successful transition to sustainable aviation. At this point in time, people are generally not concerned about the environmental impact of aviation (Gössling & Peeters 2007; Lassen 2010). Few people subscribe to the view that they should choose to fly less to reduce their environmental impact. The action required is for industry to engage with shaping a different future facilitated and cajoled by government. Government will not act unless there is public support; industry will not act unless there is customer demand. The research also found that people oppose the idea of limiting flying, particularly if it is restricted on the basis of cost. People see it as unfair if the less wealthy are priced out of the market. The key to a successful transformation is to educate the public of a better aviation system to get public buy-in and a mandate for government to lead the transformation process.

The research identified the question: in whose interest would it be to explain and describe a sustainable future for aviation? A number of passengers felt that the alternative vision should be explained to people but they did not know who might do this. Government stakeholders did not feel it was their role to promote such a radical vision. The aviation industry doubted that they could cope with such a transformation and, although they did not want to be overtly hostile to the idea, there was certainly no incentive for them to promote it. So, for now, this vision remains within the non-governmental and research communities. There is likely to come a tipping point at which concerns over climate change push emissions from aviation higher up the political agenda, opening the way to a substantive debate about sustainable aviation. This could see the emergence of governmental and industry stakeholders who start to see the value in promulgating such a vision by planning to be at the forefront of twenty-first-century aerospace.

The general insight into the role of public education in formulating sustainable policy has a number of aspects. First, in a democracy, public support is needed to give politicians the mandate to act. Second, the public cannot be expected to do the deep analysis and original thinking to craft a sustainable way forward. Third, truly sustainable policy often requires short-term restrictions and it is these immediate impacts that are likely to enter the public psyche. Overcoming this natural tendency requires promulgation of a vision of a better future to describe a coherent bundle of measures where any restrictions are packaged within a framework of improvement. Fourth, the logical argument for a sustainable solution can be complex, as whole-system analysis is required. This complexity has to be boiled down to a simple clear message for public consumption.

In aviation, public communication may include mention of the need to respond to the risks of climate change as the reason why change is even being contemplated. To break the stalemate in international aviation policy will require the right set of political circumstances in which world leaders are forced to act. Such a scenario could be a future world summit to discuss why so little has been achieved to counter climate change (McManners 2012). Delivering low-carbon aviation may be difficult for the aviation industry, but the action required by governments, working in concert, can be simple if it is agreed to use taxation of aviation fuel as the prime lever. This research shows that this lever could be enough to support the commercial case for hybrid air vehicles and open the floodgates of investment capital. It is credible to suppose that a summit of world leaders, under pressure to demonstrate progress on climate change, could agree that the restrictions that prevent the taxation of aviation fuel have not only outlived their usefulness (Keen & Strand 2007) but have become a block to progress. The scene would then be set to convene a new convention on civil aviation to work out the details of a tax on aviation fuel.

The public's demand for action over climate change may be the spur to governmental action but the message for the public with regard to aviation should be more positive than negative (Lockwood 2015). The simple message can be that the experience of flying is set to change. To travel by fast jet will become more expensive as the exemption of aviation fuel from taxation is removed, bringing it in line with the tax paid by motorists. In parallel with this, an alternative travel option will be rolled out that is slower, hosted on board spacious hybrid air vehicles. This will have First, Business and Economy classes and be a much more pleasant travel experience, particular compared with the current cramped Economy Class cabin. If you are short of time you can still travel on a fast jet but all fast-jet tickets will be expensive. The message might also link the income from taxation of aviation fuel with investment in low-carbon aviation for all. Communication expressed in these terms is overall a positive message with little mention of climate change, and deals effectively with the worry about potential unfairness. The empirical research showed that people will accept the idea of travelling slower if this is rolled out in parallel with those who travel fast paying for the privilege. This is a much more effective message than simply explaining that the cost of flying will rise through taxation of aviation fuel, which elicits a knee-jerk reaction of opposition. The policy is not going to take away your 'right to fly', but it will change the options on offer with the costs landing most heavily on those most able to pay.

6.9 Conclusions

Currently, the incorporation of 'sustainability' in policy formulation is too often a buzz word to insert rather than a fundamental change to the process of crafting policy. Governments claim that sustainability is overarching policy, without putting real substance to back it up. Industry picks and chooses elements of sustainability which improve the bottom line but steer clear of fundamental change in processes or systems where the payback is not assured. People will allow sustainability to enter their lives provided it requires little effort and does not take away something they like. As the approach to sustainability matures, it will shift to the situation where it underpins policy rather than being inserted as an add-on. It will be then that novel ideas will emerge and genuine transformational change will become possible. Aviation is likely to be one beneficiary.

This research into a sector subject to considerable inertia has shown how sustainability can be side-lined by short-term challenges and deep-seated vested interests. The sustainable solution, when it is pointed out, is glaringly obvious, but no one can see it. People are so familiar with the current system and people in the industry so tied into business as usual that the vision of a sustainable future looks totally alien. It takes time, effort and deep analysis to break through the current mindset to consider radical transformation.

The key practical insights into how to bring sustainability inside the policy process discovered during the case study research are: first, the need for long-term strategic thinking and planning; second, facilitating a dialogue between stakeholders; third, support for innovation in both technology and business models; fourth, educating the general public to generate support for necessary change. These are perhaps what might be expected, but seeing them emerge from the research process gives considerable confidence that these are the key elements to focus on.

Finally, the research demonstrated that sustainability has not yet entered into aviation policy to any significant extent. It is possible to incorporate sustainability into policy but it requires much more incisive analysis than has so far been the case. Further research will be required to test these findings and explore issues such as whether dramatic improvements in efficiency might be negated by a rebound in increased demand. In addition, further research taking a similar approach could extend out to many sectors to identify other transformational solutions to the sustainability challenge.

Note

1   This chapter was first published in the journal *Environmental Science & Policy* (McManners 2016b).

7 A vision of resilient sustainability

The foundation of the conceptual analysis which underpins this research agenda was laid in Chapters 2 and 3: identifying the fault lines at the interface between globalization and sustainability, and reframing economic policy towards sustainability. In this chapter, the theoretical analysis is resumed to take forward these concepts into a vision of resilient sustainability for people and the planet. In the future portrayed here, sustainability has become engrained in policy and the economy operates in support of people and the planet. The purpose of the chapter is to lay down an outline of a desirable end point to aim for when developing policy that might be adopted to shift society from where it is now to where we would want it to be. The detail can be disputed; it is the overall picture of a world operating successfully within planetary limits which this chapter attempts to convey. Within the confines of a single chapter, the resolution of the picture is necessarily limited. The chapter is not comprehensive in the issues discussed and the discussion of each issue is not complete. However, this vision is based on substance, including previous in-depth analysis of how the Sustainable Revolution will play out (McManners 2008) and the implications this has for policy in the real world (McManners 2010). Reality may, in the end, not live up to this vision but it is attractive, and a worthy pedestal on which to place the policy framework proposed in the next chapter (Chapter 8). It should be reasonable to assume a degree of success and allow optimism to encourage policy makers to deliver the better future outlined in this chapter rather than accept that the flaws in the current political reality are fixed constraints.

Resilient sustainability requires balanced policy for a secure future on a finite planet. Human progress via sustainable development is accepted to be an important foundation of policy by leading institutions such as the United Nations and the European Commission (Dalal–Clayton & Sadler 2014) but translating good intentions into hard policy is proving difficult. This lack of a coherent way forward is not surprising given the fault lines at the interface between globalization and sustainability outlined in Chapter 2. There is a fundamental mismatch between macroeconomic policy based on free trade, open markets and pure economic efficiency aimed at delivering growth and sustainability policy focussed on delivering social outcomes whilst keeping environmental impacts within sustainable limits. Unless this is resolved the world faces a dystopian future as resource limits are breached, environmental damage escalates and people's livelihoods are put at risk - even in the developed world where currently people feel detached from such warnings (Bandura 2007). On the other hand, in theory, Utopia is within our grasp if we deploy widely sustainable technologies - such as renewable energy harvesting - in conjunction with shifting from consumerism to focussing on nurturing real quality in people's lives. As with all complex societal change, we are likely to muddle through without arriving at either Dystopia or Utopia. However, the concept of dystopian and utopian directions for society is useful to inform discussion about policy options and possible futures (Harvey 2000; Jansen 2001; Hjerpe & Linnér 2009).

One barrier to finding solutions is that in a complex interconnected globalized world, to change anything requires everything to change. Energy systems, city design, agriculture, transport all need to change in concert. To seek to make adjustments element by element to initiate a transition to a sustainable future is proving difficult. The vision presented here is based on the assumption that policy makers can be persuaded to embrace systemic transformational change. For such persuasion to succeed, the decision maker needs an idea of the desired endpoint. Without this, every decision is a short-term response based on limited facts applied to one sector; policy is forever chasing its tail instead of leading towards a better future.

This chapter outlines a vision of the sustainable world to which humanity could aspire. It is built around the conceptual analysis presented in Chapter 3, together with insights from the empirical research. First, it should be recognized that macroeconomic policy can have a huge influence on the nature and form of world society. Second, the way that macroeconomic policy is crafted should be subservient to the higher-order policy of sustainability. Third, an appropriate policy framework within which macroeconomic policy should fit has the attributes of 'proximization', summarized as doing the rights things in the most appropriate place controlled at a level where true balance can be achieved (the concept of proximization will be taken further in Chapter 8). This vision of 'resilient sustainability' is utopian, but it is not idealistic dreaming without a logical basis; it is a cool, hard appraisal of what might be possible in an imperfect world – a 'pragmatic Utopia' where idealism is tempered by realism.

In sketching a 'big picture' of a sustainable world economy, aviation will feature as an example of how one part of the global economy will change as part of the complex network of change. In Chapter 5 a sustainable future for aviation was considered within the current macroeconomic model. Here this future for aviation is wrapped into the vision of a future where everything changes. It will be shown that some of the points of current resistance to transforming aviation are seen as much less important when the changes are viewed as part of greater change towards a sustainable world economy.

7.1 Background

Continued conformance to the market fundamentalism that underpins economic globalization will drive global economic efficiency to new heights, reaching into every corner of the world economy, mobilizing the exploitation of resources – and stripping the planet bare. Future policy could be pinned on hopes that this dystopian view is an exaggeration. Perhaps it would be possible to broker agreements that rein in the excesses of globalization whilst continuing with the model of free-market economic growth (Hirst et al. 2009), but improving governance of the global commons to the extent required would be hugely challenging (Pretty 2003). The experience of the world's attempts to reach agreement on how to deal with climate change should cast doubt on the feasibility of such altruistic coordination at global level. Giving ground for the global good is not a common occurrence in international negotiations. World leaders have more than a tendency to put national self-interest first – national interest is often the explicit aim when entering a negotiation. In such a political climate, continuation with economic globalization leads naturally to the dystopian default option of drawing on resources until they are expended. To stay on a course to Dystopia, hoping that it might be possible to take a detour some point further along the way, is a dangerous path to follow.

It would be better to have a macro economy framed by policy which, by default, tends to lead towards a utopian future. Let us consider proximization as such a policy framework. This encourages and allows people to manage their own affairs in the knowledge that people are very good at developing ways of living when empowered to do so. There will be an enormous variety of social and economic systems as people find their own way to make the best of their circumstances. The actual future is likely to be rather harsher than presented here, as people's self-interest comes to the fore, striving to build a better quality of life for their community and country. The idealism of a cooperative and coordinated globalized world would be replaced by the pragmatism of self-determination. The current international system based on globalization is flawed because it takes no account of environmental limits; a system based on self-determination is also flawed because people put their own needs and security first. The latter imperfect system is better than the former because it leads to a safe and stable future under local control, and fosters stability at the macro level because less integration reduces the risk of domino effects. The key is accepting that there will always be flaws in the management of human affairs and crafting policy that works despite them.

To be guided by the aspiration to create a new path which heads towards the Pragmatic Utopia mapped out here, is a more powerful and positive vision than going down the well-trodden path which ends in Dystopia, hoping to turn off along the way but with no map to show how.

7.2 A Pragmatic Utopia

World sustainability would appear to need a global solution and a global plan of action (Sach 2015). This leads to targets such as the SDGs and to discussions about responding to climate change by setting up a global carbon market. It should be borne in mind that real-world examples of top-down planning solutions for complex entities have a poor record of success. This was demonstrated by the central planning used by the Soviet Union and applied in China under Chairman Mao Zedong. These both had idealism at the core, but the results were disastrous. The world does not need grand plans based on idealism, but pragmatic real-world solutions. People thrive and find solutions when given the freedom to use their drive and innovation to build a better life for themselves and the people around them. Brokering a balance in human affairs at the community level is where humans excel. Not all communities will be models of success, and disputes will arise, but the mechanism of community relations can navigate a way forward that suits the circumstances the community encounters. The global component of the solution to a sustainable world is an international framework which facilitates, supports and encourages sustainable living in communities, cities, countries and regions. This vision of a sustainable world is communicated best by illustrating how it might look from the bottom up. This pragmatic utopian vision is not an idealist's view which is forever beyond reach, but an endpoint which it might be possible to get close to achieving, if not for everyone, at least for those communities that grasp the opportunities to live within the constraints of securing the long-term future.

The presentation of Pragmatic Utopia which follows has enough elements to give an impression of the complex interconnected transformation which true sustainability requires. This is necessarily illustrative rather than definitive; it is incomplete and is not a precise prediction. A more complete vision with many more dimensions is available (McManners 2008), but this vision focusses on the economy and mobility systems matching the scope of the research.

7.3 Communities

A resilient community has control of its own affairs, living within the constraints of its geography and taking advantage of the opportunities of time and place. The facilities and infrastructure work in harmony with the prevailing climate, harvesting local resources such as renewable energy. Food is predominately locally sourced and is healthy and fresh. This is not a reversion to an old-fashioned low-technology rural life style but a leap forward beyond the industrial age to an era when quality of life is the priority of policy and sustainability is engrained in the fabric of society. Looking back on the lives that people lived at the dawn of the twenty-first century, eating packaged food of uncertain source, a waste system overloaded with cheap junk and drawing energy from power plants burning coal, they will seem like the lives of paupers. There is no guarantee that the future will match this vision of better living but there are no substantive barriers to achieving it. The only real barrier is the belief that high consumption is necessary for a better life. Living better and consuming less sounds like a hair-shirt recipe for uncomfortable living. In fact, it is a sensible way forward to bring more quality into people's lives by bringing the economy back under human control to work in support of society and sustainable living.

People inhabit buildings now which are inferior to those provided in a sustainable future. Residents put up with poorly insulated homes because they can be heated (or cooled) directly or indirectly by fossil fuel. In the temperate climate of the UK it is feasible to build homes of such a quality that additional heating from fossil fuel sources is not required (Chance 2009). There would need to be a massive re-education of the building industry, and a shift in attitudes, but the technology is mature and such buildings should be standard. Such buildings are not common because of the skewed economics that make it cheaper to fit heating systems burning fossil fuel than build a structure of much higher quality. Sustainable buildings will cost more; it might take longer to pay back the mortgage or the owner will have to accept a smaller home for the loan they can afford. Currently most people in the UK do not choose such high-quality dwellings because they are not available. They are not available because the industry does not believe that people will pay the premium, and until they are widely available people have no experience of such better homes so do not know what to expect. A short-term economic perspective by builders and home owners holds the market back from making the transition to sustainable homes.

People living in other geographic locations face a different package of challenges in designing habitation that suits the climate and the availability of sustainable construction materials, but it is universally true that low-carbon buildings are healthier, cheaper to run and better to live in (Trulove 2006). Choosing sustainable homes leads to dwellings that are different, drawing on techniques that were used before fossil fuel, such as thick walls and windows positioned to let in sunlight (and/or shaded to keep it out), combined with the best of modern building technology. Again, the focus need not be on what is taken away from people but on what is given back as improvements in the quality of habitation.

In the Global South, policymakers are starting to appreciate the community benefits of enabling poor people to exercise their agency and pursue micro-level plans to increase their productivity and income (Hanlon et al. 2010). As they start to take more control of their own affairs, in places where electricity is in short supply, local officials could learn to push back against current advice from a Western perspective to build electric grids and power stations. Instead, they could focus on the key needs of refrigeration, lighting and power for laptops and mobile phones. Solar PV, with some battery backup for lighting at night, is sufficient for the task; it allows rapid progress and avoids the development stage of industrialized power infrastructure. It is such an existing legacy which holds the West back from fully exploiting renewable energy in a cost–effective manner. Developing countries do not have to take this route and can instead bounce forward to the localized renewable energy solutions which the West finds so hard to implement. This should not be seen as the West imposing restrictions on development; for example, people in such places can aspire to have luxuries such as air conditioning. There is a convenient relationship between the ambient temperature and the strength of the sun which people can exploit without the need for fossil fuel. The key issue for the less developed world is to side-step the most polluting and damaging stages of the development path of conventional industrialization.

In sustainable communities, the everyday things are of good quality and designed for longevity, with repair and refurbishment the natural choice. The manufacturing sector adopts the cradle-to-cradle approach, requiring short supply chains and a very close relationship between manufacturer and end consumer (McDonough & Braungart 2002 and 2013). Manufacturing cheap products in remote locations and shipping them across the world to end up in landfill at the end of their lives will be outlawed. Taking the concept to its natural conclusion, within an altered macroeconomic framework conforming to proximization, it becomes feasible that rubbish is made obsolete, as a sustainable system of resource use and re-use is embedded in society and the economy. Conventional economic thinking encourages a throw-away society which achieves short-term economic efficiency on the back of wasteful resource utilization. People living in a sustainable society will have fewer possessions of greater quality, which they keep for longer. It is an attractive idea to move away from the clutter of junk-filled lives to living high-quality sustainable lives. To do that in the current world would be nearly impossible as people have to accept the products and support systems on offer. The changes are not about preventing or stopping people from buying what they choose but about making better choices available.

This brief overview of community living in the future emphasizes localism. This is not localism by edict but localism because it works. People with the freedom to run their own affairs will build a wide variety of communities; some will be exemplars of good living and others examples of dysfunctional communities in need of reform. As one community celebrates success, others can observe and draw lessons to decide what might work for them and take ownership of the challenge. This is not one-size-fits-all policy coming from above, but policy tailored to local circumstances. There will be flows of resources, goods and materials where there are real needs. Resilience and sustainability come from brokering agreements with other communities close by and further afield. This requires pushing back against the idea of enforced market access, with communities free to defend their local economies. Through the lens of conventional economics, this would be highly inefficient compared with policy to maximize short-term economic advancement. There will, of course, be actors who will focus on short-term economic advantage but the stage on which they perform should be designed for stable communities in balance with a sustainable resource base.

7.4 Cities

City buildings have gone through a transformation over the last half-century with international designs migrating to all corners of the world. Impressive steel-framed buildings clad in acres of glass can be found in any capital city. New buildings in the sustainable cities of the twenty-first century will be designed around the local culture and climate using materials available in the vicinity and making maximum use of renewable energy harvesting technologies. Living in buildings will be more pleasant, drawing in natural light and using ventilation designed for both health and energy efficiency. This renaissance in city design will extend beyond buildings to the whole support infrastructure. Western cities suffer from design based on the car and the infrastructure to support the car. As cities are designed for people, the car will be demoted. Investment will flow into public transport including light rail, trams and buses. The tax regime will be soft on taxis and easy on hire cars. In this future, private cars are taxed heavily so that the people who continue to own and drive a car pay a high price for the privilege. This becomes politically acceptable because of good public transport, access to affordable taxis and the easy availability of affordable hire cars for the weekend away or trip where a car is ideal. The key change is to break down the expectation of car ownership. Such a trend is already observed amongst the young generation of city dwellers choosing not to own a car.

> Across all groups we are seeing a rise in utilitarian attitudes towards car travel, which indicates that car ownership is likely to increasingly shift towards new forms of car access, such as car hire and car clubs. An equally significant factor pointing towards more permanent changes in attitudes is the way in which use of public transport modes when young increases the likelihood of continuing to use these later in life.
>
> (ITC 2015: vii)

A city teeming with walkers, cyclists and served by good public transport is feasible now, but car use remains deeply engrained in developed societies such as the UK (ITC 2015). The legacy of the twentieth-century love affair with the car will take time to fade and replace. It may be in the cities of the developing world where most progress is made as this vision of better living pushes back against the outdated Western view which gives cars a high priority.

The key constraint on cities is space. The balance between public and private space will be key. Tight communities and cities that work at the human scale require high density, not the sprawling suburbs that were a common aspiration of the twentieth century. Families will have high-quality but limited space for their exclusive use, with larger community spaces shared with others. Instead of urban areas spreading like cancerous growths, cities will be rebuilt along sustainable lines of high-quality dense living with good air quality, drawing nature back into urban life not just through parks but also through urban agriculture, common in poorer countries, which will become a standard feature of all sustainable cities.

7.5 Transport

Emissions from transport are second only to electricity generation and in 2007 accounted for 23 per cent of global CO_2 emissions (Davis et al. 2010). The historic path which has delivered the current global transport system has been driven by the opportunities of new technology and the easy availability of fossil fuel. On the sea, the sailing clippers that dominated sea travel for a time were replaced in the nineteenth century by steam ships powered by coal, which was cheap and plentiful. In the air, as the technology of aeroplanes was developed, aviation became an important part of the international transport network, first as a niche and expensive option but now as a mass-market service. It is seen as fast and modern, requiring limited investment by governments. Airports could be built quickly relying on the private sector to invest in aircraft. On the ground, rail became the poor cousin of transportation, as road transport grew in importance, with roads built relatively quickly and vehicles provided by the private sector. The current global transport system has primary modes of fast jets, sea container transport and road transport supplemented by rail capacity. Fossil fuel is currently the main energy source for all these transport modes.

Global transportation does not conform to a top-down plan but has come about as an evolution according to economic drivers. As sustainability becomes the prime concern, it is easy to conclude, through analysis of what sustainability requires, that the future of this energy-intensive sector needs to be low-carbon. Simple logic leads to the conclusion that fossil fuel for transportation should be taxed to raise revenues to build low-carbon infrastructure. The current situation, in which there are no firm plans to limit emissions, and fuel for international aviation and international shipping is free of tax, is a block to progress. Until the transport economics is altered to make low-carbon transport commercially viable, there is no incentive to deliver the better transport system described below.

Twenty-first century transport could have rail as the backbone for long-distance national and regional transportation within continents. Where rail is electrified, there is considerable potential for this transport mode to be sustainable, provided the electricity generation uses renewable sources.

> Whether electric railways can be zero carbon depends on the source of the electricity. One possibility would be to fit solar PV collectors along the whole railway real estate which can be considerable. For example, one km of track might occupy real estate of 20m wide; that is 20,000 m² of solar capacity; capture 150 watts of electricity per m²; total energy could be 3,000Kw. That is enough to power a typical electric locomotive. There could also be wind turbines as the railway is already an intrusion into the natural environment so objections to collocation of wind turbines might

be less. Embarking on a bold project to deliver zero-carbon railway could become carbon negative because, on the rough calculation above, far more energy would be generated than required to run the trains.

(McManners 2012: 151)

High-speed rail will be attractive for longer journeys, crossing continents currently served by short-haul flights. There will also be strong demand for moderate speed rail where reliable schedules and services on board make speed less of an issue. Building additional rail capacity will require a commitment to long-term infrastructure planning and considerable investment, but this is relatively low technology within the capabilities of all countries. Embarking on building and expanding rail infrastructure will provide jobs and a boost to the local economy, as opposed to air transportation where the aircraft are the main expense and bought from global corporations based in developed countries.

For intercontinental transport, there will be resurgence in sea transportation. There is huge potential for modern sailing ships which may look nothing like the ocean clippers of the past, as engineers are given the task of designing ships running on renewable energy from wind and solar energy. Currently, fuel for ships is cheap and free of tax such that there is no incentive to give the engineers such a brief. Low-carbon shipping may be more subject to the vagaries of the weather, but slack within schedules should make this a manageable constraint and a small price to pay for much better modern clean twenty-first century shipping.

For long journeys, air travel will remain popular. Instead of all international air transport being hosted on fast jets, these will only be used where time is critical and passengers are willing to pay a high premium; for example, world leaders, senior business executives and the super-rich. Of course, richer people who are not under time pressure might prefer to travel more slowly in more comfort on a low-carbon hybrid air vehicle. The bulk of air transportation will shift to these hybrids, as explained in Chapter 5. That analysis of the future of aviation was constrained to consider a pathway starting from where aviation is now. Placing aviation within the wider context of the sustainable global economy described here reinforces the view that a revolution in aviation leads to a much better future transportation model for passengers and for the planet. Not only is such a global economy less reliant on international transportation but policy will also have been used wisely to dramatically reduce the use of fast jets in favour of low-carbon flight.

Global transportation as a complete system operating within a sustainable world economy looks very different, as the need for freight capacity and facilitating trade is less important. Tourism will remain an important source of income, particularly for those countries that decide to protect their natural assets and use ecotourism to earn income. However, as proximization encourages people to take more ownership of their locality there could be a return to taking holidays closer to home. The demand for regional travel could remain strong, with, for example, people in northern Europe venturing to southern Europe for the sun, and residents of northern states of the US taking holidays in Florida. Such journeys are well within the scope of hybrid air vehicles taking off in the morning and landing in the afternoon. These large air vehicles could have solar cells across their extensive upper surface and provide reliable cruise propulsion for daytime flights above cloud height where the sunshine is reliable. The dilemma of how to fly in the twenty-first century would have been solved. People can continue to fly, and do so with low environmental impact by flying more slowly. This is evidently a sustainable way forward, but in 2016 progress is blocked by a stalemate in international aviation policy. For as long as the aviation industry has a guarantee that that aviation fuel will not be taxed, there is no commercial basis for this next leap forward in aviation.

The particular example of aviation, singled out for attention in this research, shows that bold action to put sustainability to the fore, with priority over the short-term economic case, leads to better long-term solutions. At some point, the world will have to grasp the challenge of aviation and the longer it takes, the more investment will be wasted in reinforcing and expanding a system that will eventually see dramatic change. Making the policy choices now, or at least putting in place the intention for such change, will start the process of transformation. Such a transformation will be highly disruptive but this will be lessened the sooner the decision is made, preventing adding yet more capacity to the obsolescent twentieth-century model of aviation. When the future for aviation is viewed as part of a sustainable world economy, it looks compelling. The current aviation model may be an impressive example of what people could achieve in the twentieth century, but the future model is even more impressive and inspiring as the shift to low carbon across all transport modes delivers the transport system that fits the needs of the twenty-first century.

7.6 Conclusion

A prediction for the future of something as complex as world society and the global economy is full of uncertainty. To make a prediction assuming the continuation of the dominance of the neoliberal agenda in world affairs, based on the extrapolation of observed trends, leads to the conclusion that a further period of global economic growth is possible. It can also be concluded with a similar level of confidence that this will lead to a dystopian future of the planet stripped bare. It would be convenient to accept the first of the predictions and ignore the second, but the two predictions are linked. To reap the benefits of the model of economic growth based on an open global market will lead inexorably to exploiting resources until depletion. The vision of the future presented in this chapter relies on a different policy frame for macroeconomic policy with the characteristics of proximization. Whether this vision becomes reality depends on people's willingness to make it so. Currently, it seems unlikely that those who influence policy at global level could orchestrate such a policy reversal and scale back on support for economic globalization. Change is more likely to be initiated from the bottom up, with countries taking more control of their affairs and pushing back against advice from the World Bank and IMF. Eventually, it can be hoped that policy makers retreat from the current focus on objectives couched in economic terms to place people and the planet first. It is suggested here that optimism is justified that people will in the end choose the path of sustainability, but there may be considerable more environmental damage before macroeconomic policy is put back in its proper place as the servant of humanity to facilitate a sustainable society living on a finite planet.

8 Proximization

Delivering resilient sustainability

This chapter takes the conceptual analysis forward to consideration of a policy framework which could facilitate the delivery of the vision presented in the previous chapter. Taken in isolation, this chapter might be seen as a radical departure from what is regarded as sound macroeconomic policy. Indeed, it is a radical departure from current thinking, but in the context of the analysis and argument presented in this book, this is a logical progression of the argument. The reader should avoid the instinctive reaction to think that 'this is not how the world works' when reading the proposal. Yes, indeed, this is not how the world works. The world needs to work better, and that means working differently. The proposal presented here in support of the policy of 'proximization' should be discussed and debated, not thrown out because it does not conform to the current mainstream economic perspective.

8.1 Introduction

World society and the world economy are deeply unsustainable, with consumption high and rising, and fossil fuel dependency widespread (Victor 2010). There is little evidence of real progress towards reconciliation of economic activity with ecological sustainability within the current international policy framework (Fritz & Koch 2014). The model of a sustainable society and economy is radically different, with closed resource flows, energy harvested from renewable sources and progress measured by quality of life. The difficulty is that the transition that needs to take place in the real world will take decades to complete. The logical deduction is to shift the formulation of macroeconomic policy towards sustainability without further delay, but it will not be easy to persuade those who have an economic stake in maintaining the status quo.

World leaders and policy makers face the immediate challenge of fixing a faltering global economy alongside the long-term challenge of dealing with increasing pressure on the environment. These are seen as discrete issues requiring separate solutions. For the economy, the overwhelming focus is on maintaining growth. For environmental pressures, conferences have been convened and agreements discussed, but the degradation to the environment continues largely unabated (Schiermeier 2012; Polasky 2012). In reality, there are linkages between macroeconomic policies and the increasing environmental load. Not only is the drive for economic integration increasing the pace of exploitation of the ecosystem, but it is only a matter of time before we see the reverse effect as environmental damage impacts on the economy (Kelley et al. 2015). This could be particularly difficult as the related problem of resources becomes a major concern and continued access becomes a cause for conflict (Cramer 2002; Peters 2004; Martenson 2011; Steinbruner et al. 2012). A solution to the world's foremost challenges requires examination of both environmental and economic challenges within the same analytic frame.

It is argued here that contemporary macroeconomics has become a part of the problem, whilst it is based on the unsustainable paradigm of increasing consumption and perpetual growth. The flaws were exposed in the early 1970s by the Club of Rome (Meadows et al. 1972 and 2004) and outlined again by Tim Jackson (2009) as he argues that prosperity need not require growth. However, an alternative policy framework is slow to emerge because of the dominant adherence in international policy to support for economic globalization. The financial crisis of 2008 should have been a cause to pause and reflect but the immediate response focussed on fixing globalization rather than considering fundamental reform (Barker 2009; Chorev & Babb 2009). There is, however, some sign that support for globalization may be faltering as the systemic risks of the globalization model are better understood (Goldin & Mariathasan 2014).

To develop this alternative framework for macroeconomic policy required that assumptions of policy in support of economic globalization were put to one side to consider what a global macroeconomic framework might look like based on policy that embraces ecosystem sustainability as the overriding priority and necessary constraint for society living on a finite planet. It relies upon acceptance of the vision presented in Chapter 7 as an appropriate destination to which society should aspire.

The chapter starts with identifying the core challenge of human exploitation exceeding the ecological capacity of the planet. The subsequent sections build the argument for an alternative macroeconomic framework, starting with reframing sustainability. This leads into presenting the concept of proximization including an explanation of the assumptions used, a definition and a set of principles. Finally, there is a section identifying the consequences of adopting such a policy framework.

8.2 The challenge

The world faces the existential problem of environmental degradation as the ecological footprint of humanity has risen from 50–60 per cent of the planet's capacity in the 1960s to 150 per cent by 2012 (Global Footprint Network 2013) – and still climbing. See Figure 8.1 for a diagrammatic illustration of society's footprint outstripping the planet's capacity.

1961   **2012**

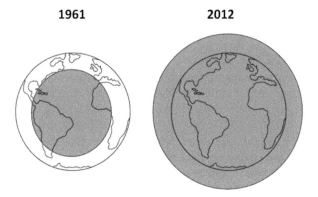

Figure 8.1 Global ecological footprint 1960–2012

Economic policy divorced from the reality of living within planetary limits has become a problem. Bridging the divide through reform to macroeconomic policy opens up the possibility of a solution.

It is contended here that the ineffectiveness of international environmental policy is, in part, due to dogged adherence to inappropriate macroeconomic policy. The narrow focus on outcomes defined in economic terms and measuring progress with economic metrics act as a straitjacket, whereas the purpose of economic policy should be to facilitate the delivery of higher objectives for society. There could not be a higher objective than global ecosystem integrity. Therefore, alterations to macroeconomic policy should be an integral component of the required changes to deliver effective environmental policy (Daly & Farley 2011).

Currently, environmental policy is often regarded as an add-on with attempts made to bring it inside the economy, but, particularly at global level, this is proving problematic (Bowen & Hepburn 2014). Ideas such as allocating a value to parts of the ecosystem and the services it provides, or establishing carbon markets to control CO_2 emissions in response to the risks of climate change, have potential. However, the analysis presented here suggests that thinking about how to bring environmental factors inside the economy can miss the most important point. The reality is that the economy has to operate within planetary limits. This truism is obvious to environmental scientists but economists have to be persuaded that the true challenge is how to reconcile economic policy with environmental policy. It is not that the economists are necessarily at fault but that politicians listen to their advice more intently than to that of their environmental scientists. Building the economy seems to have a stronger political resonance than environmental policy, but continued denial of the fundamental importance of the environment is leading society to a difficult juncture. Economists have a valuable role in developing and applying economic policy, but the narrow economic view should not be allowed to dominate policy, particularly after such a long period during which the environment has been sidelined in the pursuit of growth. It is time for environmental policy to come to the fore, not as an add-on to economic policy but as an integral component of the policy framework.

The challenge that researchers, policy makers and economists face is to install global ecosystem integrity as the basis of the overarching macroeconomic policy framework, thus holding economic policy within bounds and delivering the aspirations of sustainability. First, let us consider reframing sustainability, a term which has come to have multiple meanings, to bring back the focus to what sustainably really means in the context of thriving on a finite planet.

8.3 Reframing sustainability

A definition which captures the challenge of sustainable development is 'to satisfy present and future human needs within the limits of the biosphere ...' (Handmer & Dovers 1996: 484). The global ecosystem is now under greater pressure than at any time in human history, supporting the need for a research agenda which recognizes that the planet has limits that have to be respected as an overriding constraint on policy (Rockström et al. 2009). The other perspective that is gaining some support is that growth is not necessarily a requirement of a sound economy (Jackson 2009; Fritz & Koch 2014), and a fixation on growth may actually be a part of the problem (Buch-Hansen 2014). Objectives for society should not be about quantity but quality in people's lives within the prime constraint of living within the limits of the planet.

The challenge the world faces is a complex web of interconnected issues which includes climate change, overreliance on fossil fuel, resource limits, deforestation and biodiversity loss, to identify just some of the strands. Repeated efforts over the last two decades may have clarified the nature and difficulty of the challenge (Harris 2014) but solutions are proving to be elusive. Each candidate solution, designed to address one area of concern, ends up having impact elsewhere. For example, biofuel seemed ideal as a drop-in replacement for hydrocarbon fuels derived from oil, but this has knock-on impacts on agriculture, food production and, indirectly, habitat loss. Biofuels will be part of the future but only as part of a complex new energy web, which in turn is part of the complex web of a new economy. If there is to be a transformation of the current unsustainable world economy, there has to be structural change, particularly with regard to the central issue of replacing the fossil-fuel economy. The implementation of a global carbon market may be beneficial (Bonnie et al. 2002; Schneider et al. 2010) but such plans should not obscure the core logic that the withdrawal from fossil fuel dependency leads to a very different economy. Acknowledging this is to accept that there will be significant disruption, but remaining deliberately ignorant makes the transition harder than it needs to be.

For sustainability to become the foundation of the global economy, there will have to be radical change. What is the macro policy framework that could facilitate such a transformation? This is the central question this chapter seeks to address.

Encouraging further globalization has been the focus of macroeconomic policy since the Reagan–Thatcher era of the 1990s. The evident economic opportunities (Coe et al. 2008) have sidelined the associated problems of resource depletion and environmental degradation. It has even been suggested that

> externalisation of environmental burden through international trade might be an effective strategy for industrialised countries to maintain high environmental quality within their own borders, while externalising the negative environmental consequences of their consumption processes to other parts of the world.
>
> (Wiebe et al. 2012)

It is not suggested here the developed countries are knowingly duplicitous but it is suggested that they are attempting to address environmental challenges without questioning whether the underlying problem might be the current economic model. It is more convenient to think about sustainability overlaid on the current macroeconomic framework, but when we do that, as this researcher has been trying to do for many years, we keep hitting barriers to progress. The 'Eureka' moment, during a long and difficult struggle to reconcile the conflicting elements of sustainability, was the insight that the overall macroeconomic context is not a fixed constraint but a series of policy choices that can be changed (Blanchard et al. 2010).

It is not disputed that current policies in support of economic globalization are economically efficient, but a narrow focus on economic efficiency cannot be the basis of resilient sustainability. The policies that support globalization are designed to grow GDP and to fuel economic growth. Over the last two decades, this has been delivered, but other important factors have been pushed aside, or not been given sufficient priority. Global economic integration is widely championed, but the time has come to question such policy (Chorev & Babb 2009; Sunley 2011).

Whilst discussing sustainability, the term 'resilience' should also be considered. Sustainability and resilience are not the same (Derissen et al. 2011), but it is suggested here that they are complementary terms. A secure stable society or sound economy should ideally be both sustainable and resilient. The approach to sustainability presented here builds on the idea that there is weak and strong sustainability (Neumayer 2003; Dedeurwaerdere 2014). Strong sustainability acknowledges that natural capital is qualitatively different from manufactured capital, and putting natural capital at risk is dangerous and can have far-reaching consequences (Ekins et al. 2003). The concept of 'resilient sustainability' is presented here, based on designing the structures of the economy and society to allow a proactive response to safeguard natural capital. Drawing on the three interpretations of resilience used by Martin and Sunley (2015), a definition of resilient sustainability can be crafted:

Resilient sustainability is the delivery of quality of life in a way that safeguards the global ecosystem for the benefit of future generations, with the capability to anticipate, resist and bounce back when sustainability is threatened.

The concept of resilient sustainability is a potential game changer for policy makers but what is required to deliver resilient sustainability?

The consideration of sustainability tends to be through examination of one element, or series of elements. For example, it might be an industrial sector, a place, a region or a sector within a region. This is because of the impossibility of carrying out an analysis of the whole global economy in one grand analysis. The simplistic hope is that improving the sustainability of each element will add up to macro sustainability. This adjustment on an element-by-element basis may make improvements, but what if there are problems with the overall system? Tweaking each element will not work if a solution requires systemic change.

In considering the systemic change required to deliver resilient sustainability, it became clear during the conceptual analysis that to empower people, communities and countries to focus on quality of life in ways that safeguard the global ecosystem would require change to macroeconomic policy. To tease out what that change might be, it was decided to consider a series of assumptions about the nature of the global economy which should apply if it is to be sustainable. With the set of assumptions in place, it becomes manageable to consider what a sustainable global policy framework might look like based on the concept of proximization (McManners 2008, 2010).

8.4 The concept of proximization

8.4.1 Underpinning assumptions

The following four assumptions lay the foundations for an alternative framework for macroeconomic policy:

First and foremost, it is noted that economic globalization, for all its economic merits, regards the global environment as an externality; and it is this shortcoming which any new framework should address. Whatever else might be desired from macroeconomic policy, the prime imperative is to be able to live within planetary boundaries. The fundamental design assumption, and the reason to change what might otherwise be good economic policy, is to reduce pressure on the global ecosystem to bring the impact of human society within the bounds of what planet Earth can support now and into the long future.

Second, the fossil-fuel economy will have to be replaced by a different economy. This cannot be simply a matter of replacing one fuel source with another because the costs and availability of other energy sources do not match the current plentiful and cheap supply of fossil fuel. Different does not mean worse; the new economy should be more resilient and less dependent on risky global supply chains, as harvesting renewable energy is more dependent on making best use of the resources of the locality. This new economy will come about either because human society makes the deliberate choice to eliminate fossil-fuel dependency or because society is forced to adapt as supplies run down. The former is clearly better than the latter, because the transition can be smoother; it will cost less over the long term (Stern 2007) and it deals with carbon dioxide emissions in a more timely manner.

Third, the industrial model of extracting virgin resources to make into products which end up in landfill will be replaced by the paradigm of cradle-to-cradle manufacturing also referred to as upcycling (McDonough & Braungart 2002, 2013). This will require a circular economy of short supply chains and a close relationship between manufacturer and customer. This is a radically different manufacturing paradigm which will need to be supported by any future macroeconomic model.

Fourth, to build the new economy will require compromise between what people have come to expect and what can be provided in a sustainable manner. There are potentially difficult trade-offs to be made between what people desire and the environmental imperative. Policy makers will search out win–win situations but there is no escaping some tough choices. Global compromise, with countries giving ground for the global good, would be ideal, but the United Nations has limited power to broker and enforce such global solutions – as recent history shows (Pooley 2010). In a world dominated by national self-interest, where states hold the levers of power, reliance on global agreements looks like utopian policy. Rather than pursue the unobtainable, pragmatism should invoke national concern for security and resilience as the bedrock of policy, with each country encouraged to develop sustainable policy which matches their geography, resources, circumstances and culture.

These four assumptions underpin the development of the framework presented in this chapter: adherence to planetary limits; migration away from fossil fuel; implementation of a new paradigm in manufacturing; and the mobilization of national resilience as the pragmatic route to global security and stability.

In the early stages of the conceptual analysis, a number of mechanisms were considered to drive global change towards enhanced sustainability, including the potential of a global carbon market and ideas around enforcing sustainability into global supply chains. Each of these has fallen at the same hurdle of a lack of effective global enforcement. For a global carbon market to succeed, beyond the immediate advantages of shifting investment in the short term to where it can have most impact, the global cap on emissions must be progressively screwed tighter, squeezing carbon out of the economy. This needs to happen without leakage and to continue despite the economic pain after the easy gains have been harvested. There are similar problems with the inclusion of effective sustainability measures into world trade, requiring intrusive oversight and tough enforcement. The common problem, despite the work of the United Nations, is a lack of responsible global government with the power to broker and impose solutions. It is this vacuum at the heart of global governance which leads to defining an alternative framework which can facilitate resilient sustainability despite the lack of effective top-down direction or control.

8.4.2 Definition of proximization

> Proximization is selfish determination to build sustainable societies, aimed at social provision and driven by economic policy, whilst minimizing adverse impacts on the environment.
>
> (McManners 2008: 31)

Proximization uses the propensity of countries to pursue national self-interest, directing such efforts towards sustainable behaviours and the search for resilient solutions. Applying proximization allows and encourages countries and regions to develop economic policy appropriate to their geography, resources and circumstances with the aim of building resilient sustainable societies. The focus is on social provision, driven by economic policy, whilst minimizing adverse impacts on the environment. This should not be controversial, or perhaps very different to how sound economic policy should always be crafted, but the distinction is that instead of one-size-fits-all policy recommendations coming out of the World Bank and IMF, variety in economic models is a positive attribute of a stable global economy.

Ecosystem theory can be used as a lens to illustrate the concept. The analogy is not a precise fit but it provides a useful visual snapshot to convey the idea. Where an ecosystem is one integrated system with a small gene pool it may thrive whilst the circumstances are right and there are plenty of resources but it is not resilient and is prone to massive collapse. A resilient ecosystem has a diverse gene pool and multiple populations in dynamic balance. For a resilient global economy it should not be one integrated economy, even though when resources are ample it may grow strongly, but rather a modular system of elements with a high degree of internal self-sufficiency. If these modular elements are identical, there is still a danger that any flaw – all economic models have flaws - will propagate quickly throughout the population. For a stable macro global economy it needs to be modular in structure and have considerable variety of economic models.

To be sustainable, the global economy has to fit inside planetary limits (see Figure 8.2). Projecting business as usual, with continued global economic integration up to 2030, leads to an ecological footprint of over 200 per cent. This is patently not sustainable, equating to a failing ecosystem running out of control. Another option is to continue building an open globalized economy operating to common economic rules but to attempt to impose contraction and convergence (Meyer 2000) to then fit inside planetary limits (100 per cent ecological footprint). There is grave doubt about whether countries would ever accede to this, but even if such macroeconomic policy were possible, it would be like a monoculture ecosystem in which any flaw would be greatly

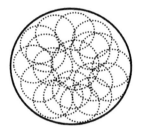 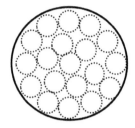 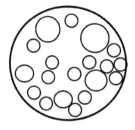

Globalized Economy [a]
(Business as Usual)

Converged Economy [b]
(Contraction and convergence)

Proximized Economy [c]
(Policy of Proximization)

Ecological footprint: 200%
Economy: High growth
Quality of life: Reducing

Behaves like an ecosystem
heading towards collapse.

Ecological footprint: 100% (+)
Economy: High efficiency
Quality of life: Low

Behaves like monoculture at
high risk of failure.

Ecological footprint: 70–90%
Economy: Low efficiency
Quality of life: High (variable)

Behaves like a biodiverse
ecosystem in dynamic balance.

Figure 8.2 Global economy 2030

Note: These represent the ecological footprints of economies inside the fixed constraint of planetary limits. (a) A globalized economy resulting from business as usual has an ecological footprint that can only be sustained over a limited period with high growth until the economy collapses as ecosystem services fail. (b) An open converged global economy would be at high risk of failure as any flaw would quickly propagate through the system. (c) A proximized global economy would be seen as economically inefficient by conventional measures but would have the attributes of a biodiverse ecosystem in dynamic balance.

amplified and the overall global economy highly vulnerable to collapse. A proximized economy is where it becomes possible to envisage a global economy operating with an ecological footprint of less than 100 per cent.

The policy framework of proximization is not radically new economic policy but simply captures and encapsulates economic common sense to overcome the flaws exposed by the world's experiment with rampant economic globalization.

8.4.3 Principles of proximization

Four principles of proximization are proposed:

1   Sustainability should be the prime basis of decision making.
2   The principle of subsidiarity should be applied.
3   The primacy of the state (as the most capable actor).
4   The use of market economics constrained to fit local circumstances.

First, sustainability should be the prime basis of decision making – balancing the economic, social and environmental consequences. It is not about social or environmental impact assessments of economic policy but about truly balanced policy in which the economic policy is designed to deliver social objectives whilst safeguarding the environment. The train of thought and analytic process of crafting resilient sustainable economic policy is quite different from trying to add sustainability as an adjunct to policy designed primarily to deliver economic ends. It requires reflection and practice before such thinking flows naturally because the simplicity of applying conventional economic rules of thumb is so attractive. In due course a new set of rules is likely to emerge but for now the economic analysis has to be based on the facts of the case, not on generalized guidance arising from a narrow focus on economic outcomes.

Second, the principle of subsidiarity should be applied. People understand their own environment, know the people around them, can take decisions for the collective good and take ownership of the result. The responsibility of running a sustainable society should, therefore, reside at the lowest possible level, with local solutions taking precedence over national solutions, national solutions taking precedence over regional solutions, and regional solutions taking precedence over global solutions. There will be challenges that require global solutions but, pragmatically, where a global solution would be ideal but cannot be delivered, national or regional solutions should be applied.

The third principle of proximization is the primacy of the state. This is where the combined value of power and commitment is greatest. Governments have power over borders, legislation and fundamental areas of policy, and can call on a sense of nationhood, loyalty and pride. They therefore have the most influence over building a sustainable society. It is an easy argument to make that national governments should take responsibility for sustainability on behalf of their people. In addition, countries with power and resources should apply their capabilities to improve environmental performance beyond their own borders. In an idealized world, this would be for altruistic reasons of world solidarity, but there is also a direct national self-interest in safeguarding the global commons. Proximization can be adopted by both left- and right-leaning governments, whose motives might be different but the outcome can be much the same in reducing damage to the ecosystem.

The fourth principle is to use market economics but constrained to fit local circumstances. This is not blind free-market fundamentalism or prescriptive controlled markets, but markets regulated to be fit for purpose, with a defined scope, geographic extent and recognition that markets work best without formal regulation (where market participants' behaviour allows it). Market-based measures are the economist's favourite tool to allow the invisible hand to act more effectively than any planning process. However, if the invisible hand is allowed free rein it can run amok. Markets need to be free to operate to find a fitting equilibrium, but also controlled sufficiently to fulfil the objectives of society and operate within appropriate limits. The ultimate market of markets is of course the global economy, the boundaries of which are the limits of the planet.

8.4.4 The adoption of proximization

The adoption of proximization requires a leap in understanding to bridge the gulf between current policy and sustainable policy. First, the nature of a sustainable world economy has to be understood. This is not a trivial task (McManners 2010; Barbiroli 2011); it requires examining hard issues such as energy, agriculture and trade, as well as soft issues such as culture and people's expectations. Second, it needs to be understood that to continue not to act, over a prolonged time period, will lead eventually to a man-made disaster, so the fact that the transition will be highly disruptive and difficult should not preclude action. Third, the final piece of the new mindset is to understand that to delay and wait until change is forced upon the world will make the transition much more difficult than it needs to be (Stern 2007, 2015; Harich 2010).

It is argued here that proximization is not so much a grand new concept but a reflection of the consequence of reining back on the policies of economic integration. Proximization is a natural rebalancing of the world order to return to a stable and effective world community. It is likely to come about because of the determination of countries to secure their future, to ensure people are empowered to defend their communities and to satisfy people's desire for a safe and secure livelihood for their family and the people around them.

Adoption of the four principles or proximization will lead in many cases to localizing activities and closing off process cycles within the local area as the only sure way of being sustainable in a resilient manner. There will still be chains of activity extending out to the regional and global level, where this is the most effective and sustainable solution. There will also continue to be commodity flows, but on a smaller scale and operating under close oversight, as countries seek to influence protection of the environment in places beyond their direct control (as concern for the global environment rises up the national policy agenda).

Resistance to the notion of proximization is expected because a key point to note, and accept in order to pursue this alternative policy framework, is that it is economically inefficient at the macro level assessed by conventional measures. Proximization requires that social outcomes and facilitating protection of the environment are higher policy objectives than simplistic economic efficiency. Pausing to reflect, it is hard to argue otherwise. Whilst the prime focus of macroeconomic policy is economic efficiency, we remain blind to the possibilities of resilient sustainability.

The hope that a sustainable future could be achieved within the current macroeconomic architecture has been dispelled by recent research by the economist Petros Sekeris (2014). He provides a deeply worrying insight into how the world might respond as resource limits are approached. He has applied game theory to the situation where shared resources are being exploited – which is the situation we have in a globalized world based on the principle of free trade. The logic is clear; the best outcome is for the players to cooperate over exploitation of the shared resource. However, Sekeris grafted onto a standard natural-resource exploitation game the possibility of appropriating the resource through violent means. He found that conflict emerges as a natural consequence. The equilibrium observed is that players exploit cooperatively the resource when it is abundant, and revert to conflict when it becomes scarce. This leads to accelerated exploitation in the period leading into the conflict. One conclusion relevant to the short term is that scaremongering over resource limits may bring forward such accelerated depletion and conflict. However, the conclusion for the long term is that early action is vital to resolve resource issues well before resource limits are reached.

World resources are still abundant and, despite weak global governance, the cooperative model of sharing resources through adhering to the principles of free trade is largely working. For how much longer will there be ample resources for the global market to draw upon? When resource limits are reached, which surely must be the case at some point in the not too distant future, how will countries respond? It is contended here that a model of proximization would engage world leaders' desire for stability and security at an early stage before resources are depleted. Although disputes may ensue, the model is designed to diffuse the possibility that this escalates into war. The merits of proximization stand up without such doom-mongering but this reinforces justification for the proximization architecture.

People closely involved with environmental issues may look favourably on the concept of proximization, but it may be difficult for such an unorthodox view of macroeconomics to enter the mainstream policy debate. Policy makers may feel uncomfortable that social objectives are not given a higher priority in this consideration of global policy. The strong alignment with ecological integrity is justified on the basis that a sound ecosystem is fundamental to any notion of long-term prosperity. Social objectives are vital to national sustainable policy but global policy should focus on that which has to be tackled at the global level. The prime focus at this juncture of history has to be to bridge the gulf between environmental and economic policy.

The world is now committed, through continued vacillation, to global warming that exceeds the levels that climate scientists regard as 'safe'. There will be an environmental tragedy; the only unknown is how serious it will be. When mainstream policy makers understand this and accept that current policy is failing, then the time will be ripe to put forward a pragmatic alternative such as proximization. Meanwhile, there is useful analysis to be done to work out the consequences, so that a viable and credible alternative macroeconomic policy is waiting in the wings when realism takes over from the utopian aspirations of those hoping to broker effective coordinated global solutions.

8.5 The consequences of proximization

This is the first time in human history that civilization has had the capability to do lasting significant damage to the global ecosystem. Accepting that current macroeconomic policy is part of the problem is the key to opening a debate that initiates the search for realistic and pragmatic solutions. 'Proximization' is a candidate for such a solution, allowing countries and regions to evolve economies that fit their geography, circumstances and culture.

8.5.1 A proximized world economy

The proximized world economy is where it would seem that a stable future is possible. This is a vibrant future of economic and cultural diversity even though at the macro level there is economic inefficiency – as measured by conventional coarse economic metrics. Such a world economy consists of a wide variety of different economies operating to suit resource availability, geography and circumstances.

In a proximized world economy, some national economies would do better relative to others in a fluid and changing relationship with economic problems localized and the overall global economy stable. This equates to a stable ecosystem with an extensive gene pool of species in dynamic equilibrium. Such a global economy consists of a wide variety of economies nestling inside planetary limits, some thriving, some contracting, and some failing. Once the concept is accepted, world institutions can develop more effective ways to step in and help struggling economies with sustainable reform. Adopting proximization delivers macroeconomic stability and makes possible reduction in pressure on the ecosystem. These are far more important to global society than a growth model divorced from planetary limits.

Adopting proximization, either as a deliberate policy choice or initiated through a number of countries acting in their own self-interest, will have wide-ranging consequences for global policy and the institutions which oversee such policy. An institution whose whole raison d'être is brought into question is the World Trade Organization (WTO). Even critics of the WTO 'rarely challenge the economic principles behind the drive to trade liberalization' (Chorev & Babb 2009: 478). The analysis presented here suggests that there is an inherent tension between the economic principle of trade liberalization and sustainability. To suggest that we should rein back on trade liberalization puts a researcher in a very lonely place, and risks accusations of economic incompetence, but this push-back against economic orthodoxy is required or it is likely that environmental incompetence will continue unabated.

There should be nothing controversial in setting high-level policy to constrain economic policy, but the difficulties arise because blinkered conformance to the perceived short-term benefits of economic globalization prevents progress, weakening the links between a society and its resource base and preventing the establishment of sustainable cycles of economic activity. Decisions are currently taken on the grounds of economic efficiency with little regard for sustainability. This should be rebalanced such that decisions are based on sustainable long-term value defined as an appropriate balance between society, the economy and the overarching imperative to live within the limits of the planet.

8.5.2 *Problems*

Taking back control of local economies through unilateral action by countries, or groups of countries choosing to withdraw from international agreements over trade and open markets, would be described as 'protectionism'. This term is often used by economists in a pejorative sense based on the view that actions which restrict trade are bad for all parties. It would be true that a world in which countries withdrew cooperation and failed to broker agreements to protect the global commons would not be a better place. However, the term 'protectionism' could be rehabilitated in the lexicon of policy if it were to mean protection of social systems and safeguarding the environment through building economies that evolve to match local circumstances. A state forced into protectionist measures through failing to compete in the global market, without applying the rationale of sustainability, would indeed suffer. However, a strong state which chose to orchestrate a proximized economy, working alongside other nations for mutual support, could retain the benefits of trade and the exchange of goods and services, not because of blanket free-trade rules but as a result of carefully crafted sustainable trade brokered for mutual advantage.

There are many issues to consider about the structure and function of proximized economies such as applying restrictions on financial flows to provide stability and the emergence of support for local currencies as a counter to the centralist mindset which established the eurozone. Much will need to be resolved through testing alternative economic policies freed from the dictate of global rules based on conventional economic thinking. It is suggested that proximization would be the beginning of a process of adopting a different mindset rather than an endpoint.

8.6 Conclusion

The central challenge the world faces is how the economy can operate for the benefit of society, now and in the future, on a finite planet. Solutions are proving to be elusive. It is suggested here that the time has come for researchers, both inside and outside economics, to challenge conventional macroeconomic theory, engage with the challenge and consider how to alter the economic and spatial models to fit inside planetary limits. This chapter presents a starting point for such research. It would be presumptuous to claim that this is a blueprint for *the* solution but if it sparks discussion with the potential to resolve the biggest challenge humanity has ever faced, it could be the start of an important debate.

Global economic efficiency should become subservient to overarching resilient sustainability policy, such that environmental limits are respected and each society is empowered to develop policy to match the circumstances of its geography. The damage human activity is inflicting on the global ecosystem is significant, and focussing on environmental agreements over many decades has failed to alleviate the risk, partly because of a blockage in macroeconomic policy. Currently, policies in support of globalization are regarded widely as the basis of sound macroeconomic policy. It might be good economics – in a world in which economic outcomes are the prime objectives – but macroeconomics should conform to higher policy objectives, in particular being able to operate within the safe limits of the planet. Proximization is presented as a proposal for a pragmatic framework which allows macroeconomic policy to conform to this higher policy objective based on four principles:

1   Sustainability should be the prime basis of decision making.
2   The principle of subsidiarity should be applied.
3   The primacy of the state.
4   The use of market economics constrained to fit local circumstances.

Proximization emerges as a natural and intuitive way to manage human affairs and would be the default basis of macroeconomics if the mantra of economic globalization had not come to dominate international affairs. Pushing back against the status quo in macroeconomic policy may not be welcome in some quarters, particularly in organizations such as the WTO, where a framework such as proximization brings into question its raison d'être. Despite the inevitable resistance, success in altering the status quo through promoting a different macroeconomic framework would open up a new avenue to limiting the damage to the global ecosystem. Further research into the potential impact of proximization on particular sectors would be useful to test this analysis and to start to tackle the difficult task of translating a conceptual framework into real-world policy.

9   Conclusions

This research examined the interface between macroeconomic policy and the world's environmental challenges. The opening premise was that to resolve the environmental challenges the world faces in the twenty-first century, of climate change, resource depletion, deforestation and other environmental damage, requires re-examination of macroeconomic policy. The research has carried out such an examination by focussing on the fault lines between economic globalization and sustainability; exploring an alternate framework with sustainability as overarching policy; and testing the ideas within the specific context of aviation. The research sought answers to three particular questions:

1   How could the formulation of macroeconomic policy be reframed to incorporate sustainability?
2   What specifically would be a sustainable policy framework as the envelope for macroeconomic policy?
3   How would it be possible to apply such sustainable economic policy?

Addressing the first two questions has generated novel perspectives and insights into how sustainability relates to macroeconomic policy. The first observation is that the dominance of economic globalization as the foundation of policy over recent decades acts as a barrier to incorporating sustainability into the management of the world's economies. Building on this entry point into the theoretical analysis, the research has added useful knowledge with an analysis of how economic policy can be reframed towards sustainability (Chapter 3). This well-grounded analysis is the foundation for a more conjectural proposal presented in Chapters 7 and 8 for a policy framework with the potential to facilitate the delivery of resilient sustainability. This framework called 'proximization' has been developed as a new way in which world affairs can be managed, pushing back against the notion of encouraging further globalization. It makes a virtue of people's propensity to negotiate a successful future for their own community, working out a sustainable balance which suits their geography and resources.

The third question was the focus of the empirical research into the real-world arena of aviation policy. This strand of the research is presented in

Chapters 4, 5 and 6. The particular methodology designed to suit this demanding research has contributed to knowledge by providing another tool for researchers termed an 'action research case study' (McManners 2016a). The action research case study identified a specific way forward for the aviation industry which is novel and original. This has broken what has until now been a policy stalemate with little sign of a solution emerging. Other useful findings from the empirical research were the general insights into how sustainability can be incorporated into policy (McManners 2016b).

The key finding coming out of this research is surprisingly straightforward and deceptively simple. It arises from challenging deep-rooted assumptions about the place that economic theory should have in discourses of sustainability. The insight which emerges, which potentially has such transformative power, is that sustainability analysis should precede building the economic model. The research has shown that this mindset can facilitate transformative solutions. In time, this may become engrained as central to policy but for now this is a radical departure from what is currently normative policy making. Bringing such thinking to the surface, and promulgating it, could invigorate new strands of research, searching for transformational solutions in other industries and other areas of policy. Sustainability could be transformed if it was not about searching for sustainable solutions which fit the existing economic models, but about designing economic models which facilitate sustainable outcomes.

The other key findings of the research are presented below, starting with returning to the fault lines identified in Chapter 2 between globalization and sustainability.

9.1 The interface between globalization and sustainability

This research commenced with an examination of the interface between globalization and sustainability (Chapter 2). The result was two sets of assumptions which encapsulate the mainstream high-level view presented in the literature. For globalization – remembering that the focus here is economic globalization - the assumptions which emerged from the analysis were:

1 Policy in support of globalization is driven by economic theory.
2 Economic policy is judged to be successful, or not, on the degree to which it delivers growth.
3 Globalization and economic growth in tandem will deliver overall a better life for the majority despite some places and some people suffering.

The research shed light on whether these assumptions do actually capture the current view, and whether they are appropriate as world society seeks to reconcile its economic and environmental ambitions. It was found that these three assumptions are indeed deeply engrained in the current mindset of policy makers. A potentially controversial deeper insight is that to allow economic theory to drive high-level policy is a barrier to sustainability. There are statements that sustainability should frame high-level policy (EU 2009b) but it was found that to follow the logic through to regarding economic policy as subservient to policy for sustainability is seen as a radical departure from standard thinking. The research has not applied much dedicated resource to examining the second assumption of growth as the measure of success of economic policy. However, in searching for the priorities of macroeconomic policy, as presented in Chapter 3, growth did not emerge as important, or even relevant. Future macroeconomic policy does not need to be pro-growth or anti-growth; it needs to be sustainable. It may be that factors such as technical innovation will allow continued economic growth within the capacity of the planet; the point is that the maintenance of growth is the wrong target. A sustainable economy may grow, it may be steady-state or it may contract; these are attributes which follow the adoption of policy rather than lead it. As we look to the future, this research shows that the assumption that growth will deliver overall a better life is not secure over longer timeframes, so policy makers should not be fixated by growth.

The assumptions about sustainability which emerged from the analysis were:

1   Human society has a long-term future.
2   Successful management of human affairs requires a balance between society, the environment and the economy.
3   We live on a finite planet and are totally reliant on its ecosystem services.

The analysis confirmed that these assumptions underpin the theoretical case for sustainability but people are slow to accept the consequences. To argue successfully in favour of the primacy of sustainability in policy requires a mindset that thinks long term; and such a mindset requires a belief that human society should have a long-term future. A minority fatalistic view was encountered in the empirical research that there is little we can do to change direction, and why should we adjust our lifestyles for the sake of future generations? If such denial of the need to take seriously the concept of a secure long-term future for society were to propagate it would undermine entirely the rationale of sustainability. The second assumption of the need for balance to deliver sustainability is widely accepted in principle and appears throughout the literature on sustainability. However, the theoretical analysis made in this research and presented in the *International Journal of Green Economics* concluded:

> Sustainable policy decisions should be balanced to deliver the needs of society in conjunction with sound environmental stewardship using appropriate economic tools. A common method of development is to start with a project proposed on economic grounds; then consult on the social issues that arise and finally commission an environmental impact assessment. Although widely used, this is an unbalanced approach. From an

economist's perspective, working with balanced sustainable policy can be frustrating because the most economic solution will often not be the most sustainable solution. This policy reversal will take time to be accepted and embedded in society. For each decision, the issue becomes how to make the most sustainable option economically viable. This is markedly different to seeking to make the most economic solution sustainable.

(McManners 2014: 296–297)

The third assumption of sustainability is that we inhabit a finite planet and are totally reliant on its ecosystem services. This is evidently true, but through the empirical research it was found that people do not see it as their job to protect it. This makes it very difficult to find the collective will to change policy that has implications for lifestyle when the beneficiary is the planet, and the planet has no power in world affairs except to the extent that people choose to take action to protect it.

Drawing together these two sets of assumptions – giving primacy to sustainability, and pushing back against the assumptions of globalization – is the basis on which the research moved forward. The difficulty of building an analysis which questions the fundamental tenets of conventional economists is described by Richard Heinberg (Heinburg 2012: 246–247):

The fraternity of conventional economists appears to be highly resistant to these sorts of challenging new ideas. Governments everywhere accept unquestioningly the existing growth-based economic paradigm, and this confers on mainstream economists a sense of power and success that makes them highly averse to self-examination and change. Therefore the likelihood of alternative economic ideas being adopted anytime soon on a grand scale would seem vanishingly small. Nevertheless, alternative thinking is still useful, because as growth ends the managers of the economy will sooner or later be forced to try other approaches, and it will be extremely important to have conceptual tools lying around that, in a crisis, could be quickly grasped and put to use.

The theoretical analysis concluded with a proposal for such a conceptual tool, which, in a crisis, could be grasped and put to use. It is depressing to conclude that it will require a crisis to force the required change, but that is the imperfect world we inhabit. The strength of the proposed conceptual framework of proximization is that it accepts the imperfections in human society and turns them to advantage. Human propensity to defend community and country can be virtuous in building a network of sustainable communities, countries and regions nestling inside planetary limits.

9.2 Proximization

> Proximization is selfish determination to build sustainable societies, aimed at social provision and driven by economic policy, whilst minimizing adverse impacts on the environment.

The theoretical strand of the research explored the rationale for the alternative policy of proximization to frame macroeconomic policy. The principles of proximization are: first, sustainability should be the prime basis of decision making; second, the principle of subsidiarity should be applied; third, the state should be recognized as the most capable actor; and fourth, market economics should be constrained to fit local circumstances. Proximization can be summarized as doing the right things in the most appropriate place controlled at a level where true balance can be achieved.

The logic which flows through the theoretical analysis, to conclude that proximization is a worthy candidate for future policy, is summarized below:

- The policies of economic globalization may be efficient (by economic metrics) over the short and medium term, but such policies do not have a safe and secure long-term future because planetary limits are left outside the policy frame as an externality.
- Over the long-term an alternative policy frame to economic globalization will be required.
- When consideration is given to such an alternative policy framework, in the context of environmental limits, sustainability becomes the overarching priority.
- As we clarify what sustainability means, and understand the consequences, it follows that macroeconomic policy should be designed to deliver sustainable outcomes.
- The empirical research confirmed the value of applying sustainability as superior policy leading to transformational solutions. This concurs with the findings of other recent research (Scoones et al. 2015).
- As the detail is examined of how macroeconomic policy should be reframed towards sustainability, it becomes clear that the key measures of success are not economic metrics but measures which relate directly to delivering sustainable outcomes (McManners 2014).
- Sustainable outcomes have true meaning in a particular context, such as a community or country, where the required balance can be brokered, controlled and delivered.
- The utopian ideal of an open and sustainable global society has to be recognized as such. The reach of global governance is limited, and what power there is should be applied to those issues which are truly global whilst providing a framework which empowers countries to find a sustainable path which suits their geography and circumstances.

Proximization may be the logical conclusion of this analysis of sustainability in a real-world context, but it is so far removed from current widely accepted ideas about macroeconomic policy that it will be seen by many as speculative in nature – and perhaps by some people as plain wrong. There will need to be further research to test and confirm the analysis by a diverse range of actors from policy makers to academics before it would be considered for implementation. In any case, this research suggests that a top-down implementation is unlikely within the current structure of global governance, as that would require action from global institutions which have been established under the remit that increased globalization is a desirable objective of policy (Peet 2003). Proximization is more likely to come about through countries testing its merits and, if successful, other countries following by taking back more control of their affairs.

In this book, proximization is presented with a degree of confidence that it is a sound response to an analysis of the key relevant factors. However, it has gestated outside the community of conventional economists and so in their eyes will be viewed with suspicion. Proximization may be regarded as speculative policy, but it is argued here that there are strong grounds to suggest that it is worthy of further investigation to explore whether it might indeed be a solution to humankind's greatest challenge of finding the restraint to thrive on a finite planet.

9.3 A sustainable future for aviation

The research also produced useful and novel insights into a possible future of aviation which were presented at the World Sustainability Forum, Basel, Switzerland in September 2015 (McManners 2015). It was known at the outset that the debate about aviation and emissions is difficult (Gössling & Upham 2009) with current discussion limited to marginal changes within the current economic model (Sustainable Aviation 2012). The new approach developed through this research focussed on the development of a truly sustainable solution. It was discovered that the dilemma is not between whether to fly or not to fly, as the current debate is framed, but between the current model of aviation or deploying a low-carbon alternative model. Sustainability would require the latter, of course. The insight which flows from the analysis is to question whether the fast jet should remain the workhorse of the industry. A new model of low-carbon aviation was proposed where the cost-conscious passenger and freight market would shift to a slower service aboard low-carbon air vehicles (which are not currently commercially viable). The fast jet would only be for time-poor people who need to travel fast. To make this sustainable solution a reality would require the economic model to change. The key economic lever that would change the commercial dynamics in favour of the proposed new model for aviation would be to introduce taxation of aviation fuel at a high enough level to drive change. This would be a simple measure, but very hard to implement because it would need change to international agreements which govern civil aviation. The rules which prevent the taxation of aviation fuel would have to be withdrawn or amended. In the current political climate, in the face of deep opposition from the US (Keen et al. 2013), it would be extremely hard to generate any political momentum to support such change.

The research showed that there is a viable model for low-carbon aviation but that it is a novel approach which does not get considered because the existing mindset is resistant to the notion of changing economic parameters to deliver sustainable outcomes. The empirical research demonstrated the effectiveness of placing sustainability as overarching policy leading to the identification of transformational solutions.

9.4 Lessons for progressing sustainability

The empirical research also generated insights into the incorporation of sustainability into policy published in the journal *Environmental Science & Policy* and reproduced as Chapter 6. The key insight is that when the approach to sustainability matures beyond a buzzword inserted into policy documents, to become the underpinning rationale, it can be expected that novel ideas will emerge and genuine transformational change will become possible. The practical insights into how to bring sustainability inside the policy process discovered during the case study research are: first, the need for long-term strategic thinking and planning; second, facilitating a dialogue between stakeholders; third, support for innovation in both technology and business models; fourth, educating the general public to generate support for necessary change. These are not necessarily new insights (Pearce & Barbier 2000; Lewis & Conaty 2012; Stern 2015), but seeing them emerge from the research process confirms that these are elements to focus on when incorporating sustainability into policy.

9.5 Limitations of the research

Limitations of the research have arisen from the decision to have separate conceptual and empirical strands. This was perhaps overambitious. An examination of macroeconomic policy in the context of planetary limits, or a study of sustainability in aviation, could each have been a complete book. However, an examination of the former without testing ideas in a real-world context would have lacked a reality check. Examining the latter without confronting the macroeconomic context would have led to the identification of marginal transitional change. Undertaking both strands has diluted the attention that could be applied to each alone but the cross-fertilization has pushed the research to be more radical than might otherwise have been the case. For example, the ideas emerging from the theoretical analysis, that sustainability should be superior policy to pure economic analysis, seems at first to be a major departure from normative thinking and therefore questionable.

Being able to demonstrate that applying this concept to aviation breaks the deadlock in conflicted policy and identifies opportunities for transformational change, gives confidence that the theoretical thinking has merit.

The two strands of the research were allowed to take their own direction so they are not close coupled, leading to an unusual book structure which may not be familiar to readers. However, any disadvantages of this are more than offset by the way the dual approach has facilitated transformational thinking about how to approach sustainability.

A particular limitation of the theoretical research was that although the first stage reported in Chapters 2 and 3 was well grounded in the literature and moved the analysis forward from firm foundations, the second stage was less certain. The analysis reported in Chapters 7 and 8 builds on the first-stage analysis, which is peer-reviewed and published (McManners 2014), but this is not yet widely accepted outside the confines of green economists. The policy framework of proximization proposed cannot therefore be presented and defended as *the* proposed framework for macroeconomic policy which embraces sustainability. The research is limited to claiming that proximization is *a* possible candidate framework to be considered for future policy. However, recent research into thinking and reasoning indicates that solutions arising from insight (as in this case) can be better than analytic solutions (Salvi et al. 2016). The 'Eureka factor' is needed to break out of a mindset that is failing us, and 'proximization' could be the 'great speculative leap' required (Kounios & Beeman 2015).

A particular limitation of the empirical research is that although the methodology of action research was applied, it has not led to immediate change in aviation policy. Despite this lack of immediate impact, the action-orientated approach has brought greater focus, depth and insight. When the objective is to broker a solution, the researcher has to confront and resolve dilemmas. With other research methodologies it may seem acceptable to record quandaries and note opposing views. It is concluded in the paper written as part of this research, and published in the journal *Action Research*, that: 'The action orientated research conveyed the strong intention to do more than observe and record and thus delivered a stronger analysis and more useful outcome than the researcher as a neutral observer' (McManners 2016a).

9.6 Further research

Proximization is presented here within a robust analytic envelope, but to the wider academic and policy community it may be nothing more than hypothetical policy which might have utility. Further research is required to fully test the concept, to assess whether it stands up to deep scrutiny. The approach that has been applied to sustainability in aviation should be repeated with other industries and other sectors to see if a picture emerges of multiple transformations. If these studies are successful, it could be the start of a wave of novel and innovative solutions as the economic parameters are changed to deliver sustainable outcomes. This may seem almost counterintuitive in a world where economic policy rules, but this research suggests that it only takes a change of mindset to turn policy formulation upside down, to be able to deliver what society needs at this juncture of human affairs.

As the world seeks to find ways to take sustainability from a concept into real-world policy, transition paths will not be sufficient (Schmitz 2015). We will need to transform current systems, processes and economic models; and we will need tools to identify what these transformations might be. This is where the 'action research case study' developed as a tool for this research could be applied to the other challenges of sustainability. This could be a rich vein of further research, applied not just in the challenge of sustainability but also in other complex and wicked challenges.

9.7 Potential impact

To what extent does this research have the potential to have an impact on the challenge of reconciling economic policy with the paradigm of sustainability? Taking the theoretical analysis and empirical research together, what do they tell us? What can we take away as overall conclusions? This section seeks to answer these questions.

The world faces a crisis as planetary limits are breached, the consequences of climate change hit home and the planet struggles to cope within the current macroeconomic architecture. 'If the world is not able to move to an economy based on sustainability criteria, it is all of us who will suffer the consequences' (Dodds et al. 2012: 281).

The solution proposed in this research is a policy framework of proximization. How each country finds a sustainable path to match its resources and geography will be highly variable. This is not Utopia, where everybody has the resources they need and the lifestyle they want. This is a sustainable world where people struggle to build the best life they can within the opportunities available to them. In other words, this is returning to the real world and backtracking from the notion that consumption can expand indefinitely, drawing on resources that are limitless. Winston Churchill wrote of democracy: 'Democracy is the worst form of government, except for all the others' (Langworth 2008: 574). It is suggested we could write the same about proximization:

> Proximization is the worst form of macroeconomic policy, except for all the others.

To implement sustainability within a globalized economy would require extraordinarily effective global governance. There is little sign that global governance could be improved to the extent required or that people could behave as global citizens to support such arrangements. Even if it were possible to construct a functioning global economy which was fair and equitable to everyone, any flaw would quickly propagate throughout the system. As was argued in Chapter 8, stable macroeconomics requires a variety of economic models nestling together providing a resilient and sustainable system at the macro level where local weakness does not upset the whole system.

The action research case study into aviation shows how aviation could be transformed, but more importantly, it shows that transformation is possible even in this most difficult and conflicted area of policy. Aviation could be used as a barometer of when the world decides to take substantive action. Pushing for change in aviation, and succeeding, could be the start of an avalanche of change as people adopt a different mindset. We can do this, if we put sustainability at the top of the policy agenda and allow it to dominate our decision-making processes. For aviation, it needs global agreement to tax aviation fuel to deliver an economic model which supports the transformation to low-carbon flight. As an administrative procedure, this would be very simple but the political task of agreeing to do it is herculean.

Throughout this research the focus has been on logical analysis avoiding political issues. Capitalism has also not come into the firing line of the analysis. It would seem that capitalism is not the problem. The problem is the way economic globalization has come to dominate the current world order. In fact, capitalism may well come to the world's rescue when society takes back control through the nation state asserting its authority to find a sustainable path for its people. For the aviation industry, the current players see little sign that world leaders will agree to change the rules so the high-emission model of twentieth century aviation continues to expand. When governments change the rules, the venture capitalists will pour money into building aviation fit for the twenty-first century and parts of the current industry will be bankrupted. This is how capitalism can drive change. Even big aircraft makers like Boeing and Airbus may seek insolvency protection as their current models become obsolete earlier than expected within the current business plan. Their expertise, knowledge and knowhow will rise out of the disruption and reform into the aviation corporations needed for the future. Capitalism is not the problem, but it needs undiluted commitment to sustainability at the political level to unleash the power of the capitalist machine to support society in its challenge.

9.8 Reflections

Calls for action to address the world's environmental challenges are growing, ranging from popular impassioned pleas (Klein 2014) to well-argued appeals for change from economists (Helm 2012; Stern 2015) and analysis focussed on geographical aspects of sustainability transition processes (Truffer et al. 2015). So far, solutions seem to be beyond the grasp of academics and policy makers. It is hoped that this research has contributed in some way to identifying a direction that might prove fruitful as the search continues for ways to resolve the greatest challenge humankind has ever faced.

It was interesting that in the later stages of the research, the author attended the Sustainability World Forum, Basel, Switzerland (7–9 September 2015).

This was to present the results from the aviation case study (McManners 2015). There were multiple streams across the multiple discourses of sustainability, and this author could engage in and contribute to any of them. In this massively cross-discipline area there are very few people attempting to assimilate all aspects to build up the bigger picture. To be that person entering debates without blinkers is both interesting and challenging. It is interesting to see the inherent contradictions to which silo thinking leads, such as those contained within the set of 17 Sustainable Development Goals. There will have to be trade-offs, and a secure view of the bigger picture will be required to make those trade-offs. It is challenging because it is impossible to become familiar with all the different nuanced positions within a particular silo. The massively cross-discipline researcher has to be selective in what to consider in looking for truth amongst a range of opinion. That selection process of what is important and what is less important is itself subject to the prejudice and opinion of the researcher.

The current macroeconomic policy prescription in support of economic globalization, which dominates world institutions, has attracted considerable political momentum under the ill-defined banner of neoliberalism. To push back against such policy is not only to seek to change to how macroeconomics is managed but also pushes back against the political free-market movement which the US and the UK have championed for a number of decades. The mindset that underpins such policy is deep-rooted. To challenge such economic and political orthodoxy can be expected to generate opposition from those schooled to believe that economic policy, designed to deliver against economic metrics, trumps other policy objectives. A way has to be found to shift this mindset to one in which sustainability has primacy. This research has uncovered a basis on which to build such a mindset, tested it in a real-world policy context and found that it can work. However, the research also found that promulgating this mindset to other people is a slow process. People can follow the logic and be persuaded of the validity of the alternative viewpoint, but acceptance that it might be possible to change the world economic system is lacking.

The degree of interconnectedness and interdependence of the modern economy is now so great that changing anything can have consequences which cascade through the system without certainty of the final outcome. This can make us wary of change because we cannot be sure where it will take us. This makes sustainability particularly challenging because we cannot make piecemeal changes to individual elements considered in isolation. To effect the essential changes required to transition to sustainable living, we have to accept that everything changes. This is a challenge we should welcome and embrace, but it will bring disruption and it is human nature to be concerned when familiarity with a system we understand is replaced with uncertainty.

This understandable fear of an uncertain future is why we need visions of sustainable living presented as a better future. In this book, Chapter 7 serves that purpose in arguing for change in how we frame macroeconomic policy. At the sector level, the vision of sustainable aviation presented in Chapter 5 serves to garner support for a radical shake-up of aviation. These visions are not predictions and should not be used as predictions. These are credible possible futures in which optimism has been allowed space to grow. They might be over-optimistic when viewed through the lens of cool hard appraisal, but without such optimism it is hard to gain support for breaking the denial of the need for radical transformation.

An early draft of this manuscript was shared with someone who had been closely involved with previous studies into sustainable aviation which had ended in stalemate. His initial response was to rattle off a list of reasons why my vision would not work. Hybrid air vehicles could not be deployed as I had envisioned because flying relatively low and slow would make them a terrorist target; at low level the engine noise might be more intrusive for people under the flight path; and being affected more by weather such as head winds would make scheduling less reliable. Of course, these are all important issues but there are potential solutions, if we decide to push forward and look for them. Hybrid air vehicles can be made robust and more resilient to terrorist action than aircraft; the engines can be quiet, much quieter than conventional jet aircraft; and scheduling can have inbuilt flexibility for most climatic conditions. The previous researcher acting as an observer had accepted the view which permeates the aviation industry that radical change is not possible. Tacit defence of the status quo by looking for the reasons why something can't be done is human frailty. To make progress with sustainability we have to be stronger and break out of our comfort zone using radical free thinking, pushing back against those who say it can't be done.

People believe that the economy comes first and that economic metrics have priority because that is what dominates economic and political commentary. To suggest otherwise, at this point in human affairs, is quickly put aside as not credible and not relevant to mainstream policy. It requires the depth of insight that comes with reading this entire book to be persuaded of the case for change. It will take time for a cohort of influential and respected people to appreciate the argument that has been made in this research and start to reset the ruling mindset. This author has adopted the alternative mindset presented here, and through its lens the future for humanity looks bright and solutions to environmental challenges appear to be feasible. Continuing with orthodox macroeconomic policy will reinforce the current direction of the economy towards ever more consumption and ever more environmental degradation. The new direction proposed in this research, where economics is brought back as a facilitating function for higher policy objectives, may be bold and ambitious, but on close analysis is nothing more than allowing common sense to prevail.

References

Altrichter, H., Kemmis, S., McTaggart R. and Zuber-Skerritt, O. (2002). The concept of action research, *Learning Organisation*, 9(3): 125–131; republished in Volume II of Cooke, B. and Cox, J.W. (eds), *Fundamentals of Action Research*, London: Sage Publications, 101–113.

Argyris, C. and Schön, D.A. (2005). Participatory action research and action science compared: a commentary, *American Behavioral Scientist*, 32(5): 612–623; republished in Volume II of Cooke, B. and Cox, J.W. (eds), *Fundamentals of Action Research*, London: Sage Publications, 137–147.

Ayres, R.U. (1998). *Turning Point: The end of the growth paradigm*, London: Earthscan.

Ayres, R.U. (2006). Turning point: the end of exponential growth? *Technological Forecasting and Social Change*, 73(9), 1188–1203.

Ayres, R.U., van den Berrgh, J. and Gowdy, J. (2001). Strong versus weak sustainability, *Environmental Ethics*, 23(2), 155–168.

Ayres, R.U. and Warr, B. (2010). *The Economic Growth Engine: How energy and work drive material prosperity*, Cheltenham: Edward Elgar.

Ayuso, S., Rodríguez, M.A. and Ricart, J.E. (2006). Using stakeholder dialogue as a source for new ideas: a dynamic capability underlying sustainable innovation, *Corporate Governance*, 6(4), 475–90.

Bagwell, K. and Staiger, R.W. (2001). The WTO as a mechanism for securing market access property rights: implications for global labor and environmental issues, *Journal of Economic Perspectives*, 15(3), 69–88.

Bandura, A. (2007). Impeding ecological sustainability through selective moral disengagement. *International Journal of Innovation and Sustainable Development*, 2(1), 8–35.

Barbier, E. (2010). *A Global Green New Deal: Rethinking the economic recovery*, Cambridge: Cambridge University Press.

Barbiroli, G. (2011). Economic consequences of the transition process toward green and sustainable economies: costs and advantages, *International Journal of Sustainable Development & World Ecology*, 18(1), 17–27.

Barker, T. (2009). Will the reconstruction of the global economy be positive for mitigating climate change? In A. Giddens, S. Latham and R. Liddle (eds), *Building a Low Carbon Future: The politics of climate change*, London: Policy network, 21–31, [available at: http://politicsofclimatechange.files.wordpress.com/2009/06/building-a-low-carbon-future-pamphlet-web.pdf; accessed 29 March 2016].

Barnet, R. and Cavanagh, J. (2001). Electronic money and the casino economy. In E. Goldsmith and J. Mander (eds), *The Case Against the Global Economy: And for a Turn Towards Localization*, London: Earthscan, 58–69.

Barr, S. (2012). *Environment and Society: Sustainability, policy and the citizen*, Farnham: Ashgate.

Barrow, C. (2006). *Environmental Management for Sustainable Development*, Abingdon: Routledge.

Bartelmus, P. (2009). The cost of natural capital consumption: accounting for a sustainable world economy, *Ecological Economics*, 68, 1850–1857.

Bartelmus, P. (2010). Use and usefulness of sustainability economics, *Ecological Economics*, 69, 2053–2055.

Baumgärtnera, S. and Quaasc, M. (2010). What is sustainability economics? *Ecological Economics*, 69(3), 445–450.

Bergman, M. (2015). Opening Address to the 5th World Sustainability Forum, Basel, Switzerland 7–9 September.

Bhagwati, B. (2004). *In Defense of Globalization*, Oxford: Oxford University Press.

Blanchard, O., Dell'Ariccia, G. and Mauro, P. (2010). Rethinking macroeconomic policy, *Journal of Money, Credit and Banking*, 42, 199–215.

Bonnie, R., Carey, M. and Petsonk, A. (2002). Protecting terrestrial ecosystems and the climate through a global carbon market, *Philosophical Transactions A*, 360, 1853–1873.

Bowen, J. (2000). Airline hubs in Southeast Asia: national economic development and nodal accessibility, *Journal of Transport Geography*, 8(1), 25–41.

Bowen, A. and Hepburn, C. (2014). Green growth: an assessment, *Oxford Review of Economic Policy*, 30(3), 407–422.

Boyd, E., Osbahr, H., Ericksen, P.J., Tompkins, E.L., Lemos, M.C. and Miller, F. (2008). Resilience and 'climatizing' development: examples and policy implications, *Development*, 51(3), 390–396.

Boyd, J. and Banzhaf, S. (2007). What are ecosystem services? The need for standardized environmental accounting units, *Ecological Economics*, 63(2), 616–626.

Bradbury, H. (2013). Action Research: The journal's purpose, vision and mission, *Action Research*, 11(1), 3–7.

Bridger, R. (2013). *Plane Truth: Aviation's Real Impact on People and the Environment*, London: Pluto Press.

Brockington, D. (2012). A radically conservative vision? The challenge of UNEP's towards a green economy, *Development and Change*, 43(1), 409–422.

Brown, K. (2014). Global environmental change: a social turn for resilience? *Progress in Human Geography*, 38(1), 107–117.

Buch-Hansen, H. (2014). Capitalist diversity and de-growth trajectories to steady-state economies, *Ecological Economics*, 106, 167–173.

Canuto, O. and Leipziger, D.M. (eds) (2012). *Ascent after decline: Regrowing global economies after the great recession*, Washington, DC: World Bank Publications.

Carson, R. (1962). *Silent Spring*, Boston: Houghton Mifflin.

Cavanagh, J. and Mander, J. (2004). *Alternatives to Economic Globalization: A Better World Is Possible*, 2nd Edition, San Francisco: Berrett-Koehler.

CBO (2005). Options for strategic military transportation system, Congressional Budget Office Study, Washington, DC: Congress of the United States.

Ceruti, A. and Marzocca, P. (2014). Conceptual approach to unconventional airship design and synthesis, *Journal of Aerospace Engineering*, 27(6).

Chance, T. (2009). Towards sustainable residential communities: the Beddington Zero Energy Development (BedZED) and beyond, *Environment & Urbanization*, 21(2), 527–544.

Chorev, N. and Babb, S. (2009). The crisis of neoliberalism and the future of the international institutions: a comparison of the IMF and the WTO, *Theory and Society,* 38: 459–484.

Christensen, T. and Lægreid, P. (2007). The whole-of-government approach to public sector reform, *Public Administration Review,* 67(6), 1059–1066.

Coe, N.M., Dicken, P. and Hess, M. (2008). Global production networks: realizing the potential, *Journal of Economic Geography,* 8(3), 271–295.

Coghlan, D. and Brannick, T. (2000). *Doing Action Research in your Own Organisation,* London: SAGE.

Cowling, K. and Tomlinson, P.R. (2011). Post the 'Washington Consensus': economic governance and industrial strategies for the twenty-first century, *Cambridge Journal of Economics,* 35, 831–852.

Cramer, C. (2002). Homo economicus goes to war: methodological individualism, rational choice and the political economy of war, *World Development* 30(11), 1845–1864.

Crotty, J. (2009). Structural causes of the global financial crisis: a critical assessment of the 'new financial architecture', *Cambridge Journal of Economics,* 33(4), 563–580.

Crutzen, P.J. (2006). The anthropocene. In E. Ehlers and T. Krafft (eds), *Earth System Science in the Anthropocene,* New York: Springer: 13–18.

Dalal-Clayton, B. and Sadler, B. (2014). *Sustainability Appraisal: A sourcebook and reference guide to international experience,* Abingdon: Routledge.

Daley, B. (2010). *Air Transport and the Environment,* Farnham: Ashgate.

Daly, H.E. (1977). *Steady-State Economics,* San Francisco: W.H. Freeman.

Daly, H.E. (1990). Toward some operational principles of sustainable development, *Ecological Economics,* 2(1), 1–6.

Daly, H.E. and Farley, J. (2011). *Ecological Economics,* 2nd edition (1st edition 2004), Washington, DC: Island Press.

Dauvergne, P. (2010). The problem of consumption, *Global Environmental Politics,* 10(2), 1–10.

Davis, S.J., Caldeira, K. and Matthews, H.D. (2010). Future CO_2 emissions and climate change from existing energy infrastructure, *Science,* 329(5997), 1330–1333.

Davoudi, S. (2001). Planning and the twin discourses of sustainability. In A. Layard, S. Davoudi and S. Batty (eds), *Planning for a sustainable Future,* London: Spon, 81–83.

De Cock, C., Cutcher, L. and Grant, D. (2012). Finance capitalism's perpetually extinguished pasts: exploring discursive shifts 2007–2011, *Culture and Organization,* 18(2), 87–90.

Dedeurwaerdere, T. (2014). *Sustainability Science for Strong Sustainability,* Cheltenham: Edward Elgar.

Demeritt, D. (2011). The antonymies of sustainable development: sustaining what, how and for whom. In A. Leyshon, R. Lee, L. McDowell and P. Sunley (eds), *The SAGE Handbook of Economic Geography,* London: SAGE, 231–241.

Derissen, S., Quaas, M.F. and Baumgärtner, S. (2011). The relationship between resilience and sustainability of ecological-economic systems, *Ecological Economics,* 70, 1121–1128.

Diedrich, A., Upham, P., Levidow, L. and van den Hove, S. (2011). Framing environmental sustainability challenges for research and innovation in European policy agendas, *Environmental Science & Policy,* 14, 935–939.

Dietz, R. and O'Neill, D. (2013). *Enough Is Enough: Building a Sustainable Economy in a World of Finite Resources,* Abingdon: Routledge.

Dodds, F., Strauss, M. and Strong, M. (2012). *Only One Earth: The long road via Rio to sustainable development*, Abingdon: Routledge.

Ekins, P. and Speck, S. (1999). Competitiveness and exemptions from environmental taxes in Europe, *Environmental and Resource Economics*, 13, 369–396.

Ekins, P., Simon, S., Deutsch, L., Folke, C. and De Groot, R. (2003). A framework for the practical application of the concepts of critical natural capital and strong sustainability, *Ecological Economics*, 44, 165–185.

EU (2009a). The High-Level Group on Financial Supervision in the EU: report, chaired by J. De Larosière, Brussels: European Commission.

EU (2009b). *Mainstreaming Sustainable Development into EU Policies: 2009 Review of the European Union Strategy for Sustainable Development*, Commission of the European Communities, Brussels.

Evans, A.D. (2014). Comparing the impact of future airline network change on emissions in India and the United States, *Transportation Research Part D: Transport and Environment*, 32, 373–386.

Ewing, B., Moore, D., Goldfinger, S., Oursler, A., Reed, A. and Wackernagel, M. (2010). *The Ecological Footprint Atlas 2010*, Oakland, CA: Global Footprint Network.

Ewing, B., Reed, A., Galli, A., Kitzes, J. and Wackernagel, M. (2010). *Calculation Methodology for the National Footprint Accounts, 2010 Edition*, Oakland, CA: Global Footprint Network.

Financial Crisis Inquiry Commission (2011). The financial crisis inquiry report: final report of the national commission on the causes of the financial and economic crisis in the United States, [available from: http://cybercemetery.unt.edu/archive/fcic/20110310173545/http://c0182732.cdn1.cloudfiles.rackspacecloud.com/fcic_final_report_full.pdf; accessed 29 March 2016].

Findlay, R. (1990). The triangular trade and the Atlantic economy of the eighteenth century. *Essays in International Finance*, No. 177, Princeton, NJ: International Finance Section, Department of Economics, Princeton University.

Forester, J. (2013). On the theory and practice of critical pragmatism: Deliberative practice and creative negotiations, *Planning Theory*, 12(1): 5–22.

Frieden, J.A. (2006). *Global Capitalism: Its fall and rise in the twentieth century*, New York: W.W. Norton & Co.

Friedman, B.M. (2005). *The Moral Consequences of Economic Growth*, New York: Alfred A. Knopf.

Fritz, M. and Koch, M. (2014). Potentials for prosperity without growth: ecological sustainability, social inclusion and the quality of life in 38 countries, *Ecological Economics*, 108, 191–199.

Frohan, M.A., Sashkin, M. and Kavanagh M.J. (1976). Action-research as applied to organization development, *Organization and Administration Science*, 7(1/2), 129–161; republished in Volume II of Cooke, B. and Cox, J.W. (eds), *Fundamentals of Action Research*, London: Sage Publications: 367–405.

Fullbrook, E. (2010). How to bring economics into the 3rd millennium by 2020, *Real-World Economics Review*, 54, 89–102.

Gallopín, G., Jiménez Herrero, L.M. and Rocuts, A. (2014). Conceptual frameworks and visual interpretations of sustainability, *International Journal of Sustainable Development*, 17(3), 298–326.

Glennie, J. (2008). *The Trouble with Aid: Why less could mean more for Africa*, London: Zed Books.

Global Footprint Network (2012). *The National Footprint Accounts, 2011 Edition,* Oakland, CA: Global Footprint Network.

Global Footprint Network (2013). *The National Footprint Accounts, 2012 Edition,* Oakland: Global Footprint Network, [available from: www.footprintnetwork.org/ images/article_uploads/National_Footprint_Accounts_2012_Edition_Report.pdf; accessed 30 March 2016].

Godfray, H.C.J., Beddington, J.R., Crute, I.R., Haddad, L., Lawrence, D., Muir, J.R., Pretty, J., Robinson, S., Thomas, S.M. and Toulmin, C. (2010). Food security: the challenge of feeding 9 billion people, *Science*, 327(5967), 812–818.

Goldin, I. and Mariathasan, M. (2014). *The Butterfly Defect: How globalization creates systemic risks and what to do about it,* Princeton, NJ: Princeton University Press.

Gollier, C., Jullien, B. and Treich, N. (2000). Scientific progress and irreversibility: an economic interpretation of the 'precautionary principle', *Journal of Public Economics*, 75(2), 229–253.

Gore, C. (2000). The rise and fall of the Washington Consensus as a paradigm for developing countries, *World Development*, 28(5), 789–804.

Gössling, S. and Peeters, P. (2007). 'It does not harm the environment!' An analysis of industry discourses on tourism, air travel and the environment, *Journal of Sustainable Tourism*, 15(4), 402–417.

Gössling, S. and Upham, P. (eds) (2009). *Climate Change and Aviation: Issues, challenges and solutions,* London: Earthscan.

Gowdy, J.M. (1994). Coevolutionary economics: the economy, *Society and the Environment,* Boston: Kluwer.

Griggs, D., Stafford-Smith, M., Gaffney, O., Rockström, J., Öhman, M.C., Shyamsundar, P. and Noble, I. (2013). Policy: Sustainable development goals for people and planet, *Nature*, 495(7441), 305–307.

Grubesic, T.H. and Matisziw, T.C. (2012). World cities and airline networks. In P. Derudder, M. Hoyler and P.J. Taylor (eds), *The International Handbook of Globalization and World Cities,* Cheltenham: Edward Elgar, 97–116.

Guest, G., Bunce, A. and Johnson, L. (2006). How many interviews are enough? An experiment with data saturation and variability, *Field Methods*, 18(1), 59–62.

Gustavsen, B. (2008). Action research, practical challenges and the formation of theory, *Action Research*, 6(4), 421–437.

Gutés, M.C. (1996). The concept of weak sustainability, *Ecological Economics*, 17(3), 147–156.

Hall, N., Taplin, R. and Goldstein, W. (2010). Empowerment of individuals and realization of community agency: applying action research to climate change responses in Australia, *Action Research*, 8(1), 71–91.

Hall, P.A. and Lamont, M. (eds) (2013). *Social Resilience in the Neoliberal Era,* Cambridge: Cambridge University Press.

Handmer, J.W. and Dovers, S.R. (1996). A Typology of Resilience: Rethinking Institutions for Sustainable Development, *Organization & Environment*, 9, 482–11.

Hanlon, J., Barrientos, A. and Hulme, D. (2010). *Just Give Money to the Poor: The development revolution from the global South,* Boulder, CO: Kumarian Press.

Harich, J. (2010). Change resistance as the crux of the environmental sustainability problem, *System Dynamics Review*, 26(1), 35–72.

Harris, P.G. (ed.) (2014). *Routledge Handbook of Global Environmental Politics,* Abingdon: Routledge.

Harvey, D. (2000). *Spaces of Hope,* Berkeley, CA: University of California Press.

Harvey, D. (2007). In what ways is 'the new imperialism' really new? *Historical Materialism*, 15, 57–70.

Hausmann, R., Rodrik, D., and Velasco, A. (2008). 'Growth diagnostics'. In N. Serra and J.E. Stiglitz (eds), *The Washington Consensus Reconsidered: Towards a new global governance*, Oxford: Oxford University Press, 324–355.

Heinberg, R. (2012). *The End of Growth: Adapting to our New Economic Reality*, Forest Row: Clairview.

Helm, D. (2012). *The Carbon Crunch: How We're Getting Climate Change Wrong - and How to Fix it*, Newhaven, CT: Yale University Press.

Hirst, P., Thompson, G. and Bromley, S. (2009). *Globalization in question*. 3rd edition, Cambridge: Polity Press.

Hjerpe, M. and Linnér, B.O. (2009). Utopian and dystopian thought in climate change science and policy, *Futures*, 41(4), 234–245.

HM Treasury (2009). *Reforming Financial Markets*, Presented to Parliament by the Chancellor of the Exchequer by Command of Her Majesty, July 2009, London: The Stationary Office, [available at: https://www.gov.uk/government/uploads/system/uploads/attachment_data/file/238578/7667.pdf; accessed 30 March 16].

Holloway, S. (2008). *Straight and Level: Practical Airline Economics*, 3rd edition, Aldershot: Ashgate.

Hooper, P. (2005). The environment for Southeast Asia's new and evolving airlines, *Journal of Air Transport Management*, 11(5), 335–347.

Hopwood, B., Mellor, M. and O'Brien, G. (2005). Sustainable Development: mapping different approaches, *Sustainable Development*, 13(1), 38–52.

Horn, R.E. and Weber, R.P. (2007). *New tools for resolving wicked problems: Mess mapping and resolution mapping processes*, Watertown, MA: Strategy Kinetics LLC, [available at: www.strategykinetics.com//New_Tools_For_Resolving_Wicked_Problems.pdf; accessed 30 March 16].

Howarth, R.B. and Farber, S. (2002). Accounting for the value of ecosystem services, *Ecological Economics*, 41(3), 421–429.

Hudson, R. (2010). Resilient regions in an uncertain world: wishful thinking or practical reality? *Cambridge Journal of Regions, Economy and Society*, 3, 11–26.

Hummels.D. (2007). Transportation costs and international trade in the second era of globalization, *Journal of Economic Perspectives*, 21(3), 131–154.

Hynes, W., Jacks, D.S. and O'Rourke, K.H. (2012). Commodity market disintegration in the interwar period, *European Review of Economic History*, 16(2), 119–143.

IATA (2014). *Annual Review 2014*, International Air Transport Association (IATA), [available at: https://www.iata.org/about/Documents/iata-annual-review-2014.pdf; accessed 15 July 2016].

ICAO (2006). *Convention on International Civil Aviation*, Document 7300/9, Montréal: International Civil Aviation Organization (ICAO).

ICAO (2010a). *Statement from the International Civil Aviation Organization (ICAO) to the Thirty-Third Session of the UNFCCC Subsidiary Body for Scientific and Technological Advice (SBSTA33) (30 November to 4 December 2010 – Cancun, Mexico)*, [available at: www.icao.int/environmental-protection/Documents/STATEMENTS/sbsta-33.pdf; accessed 29 June 2016].

ICAO (2010b). *ICAO Environmental Report 2010*, [available at: www.icao.int/environmental-protection/Documents/Publications/ENV_Report_2010.pdf; accessed 29 June 2016].

ICAO (2013). Report of the Executive Committee on agenda Item 17 (section on climate change), Doc. A38-WP/430/P44 dated 3 October 2013, [available at: www.icao.int/Meetings/a38/Documents/WP/wp430_en.pdf; accessed 30 March 2016].

Ietto-Gillies, G. (2011). The role of transnational corporations in the globalisation process. In J. Michie (ed.), *The Handbook of Globalisation*, 2nd edition, Cheltenham: Edward Elgar, 173–184.

IMF (2000). Recovery from the Asian Crisis and the Role of the IMF, [available at: www.imf.org/external/np/exr/ib/2000/062300.htm#II; accessed 30 March 2016].

ITC (2015). On the move: exploring attitudes to road and rail travel in Britain, London: Independent Transport Commission, [available at: www.theitc.org.uk/wp-content/uploads/2015/07/ITC-ORR-Road-Rail-Attitudinal-Report-Final.pdf; accessed 30 March 2016].

Jackson, T. (2009). *Prosperity without Growth: Economics for a finite planet*, London: Earthscan.

Jacoby, J. and Cooper, E. (2012). The cultural context in sustainable development: Approaches to support the 4th pillar. In R. Amoeda, S. Lira and C. Pinheiro (eds), *Heritage 2012: Heritage and Sustainable Development*, Barcelos, Portugal: Green Lines Institute, 1209–1218.

Jacques, M. (2009). *When China Rules the World: The Rise of the Middle Kingdom and the End of the Western World*, London: Allen Lane.

Jansen M.A. (2001). A future of surprises. In L.H. Gunderson (ed.), *Panarchy: Understanding transformations in human and natural systems*, Washington DC: Island Press, 241–260.

Jones, C.I. (2002). *Introduction to Economic Growth*, New York: Norton & Co.

Joseph, J. (2013). Resilience as embedded neoliberalism: a governmentality approach. *Resilience*, 1(1), 38–52.

Kates, R.W. (2010). Readings in sustainability science and technology, CID Working Paper No. 213, Center for International Development, Harvard University, [available at: www.hks.harvard.edu/var/ezp_site/storage/fckeditor/file/pdfs/centers-programs/centers/cid/publications/faculty/wp/213.pdf; accessed 30 March 2016].

Keen, M. and Strand, J. (2007). Indirect taxes on international aviation, *Fiscal Studies*, 28(1), 1–41.

Keen, M., Parry, I. and Strand, J. (2013). Planes, ships and taxes: charging for international aviation and maritime emissions, *Economic Policy*, 28(76), 701–749.

Kelley, C.P., Mohtadi, S., Cane, M.A., Seager, R. and Kushnir, Y. (2015). Climate change in the Fertile Crescent and implications of the recent Syrian drought. *Proceedings of the National Academy of Sciences*, 112(11), 3241–3246.

Kemeny, T. (2011). Are international technology gaps growing or shrinking in the age of globalization? *Journal of Economic Geography*, 11, 1–5.

Kennet, M. and Heinemann, V. (2006). Green E=economics: setting the scene. Aims, context, and philosophical underpinning of the distinctive new solutions offered by Green Economics, *International Journal of Green Economics*, 1(1/2), 68–102.

Khoury, G.A. (2012). *Airship Technology*, Cambridge Aerospace Series Vol. 10, 2nd edition, Cambridge: Cambridge University Press.

Klein, N. (2014). *This Changes Everything*, London: Allen Lane.

Kolka, A. and Tulderb, van R. (2010). International business, corporate social responsibility and sustainable development, *International Business Review*, 19(2), 119–125.

Kounios, J. and Beeman, M. (2015). *The Eureka Factor: Aha moments, creative insight, and the brain*, London: Random House.

Kuznets, S. (1934). *National Income, 1929–1932,* 73rd US Congress, Senate document no. 124, 7.

Kvale, S. (2007). *Doing Interviews*, London: SAGE.

Langworth, R.M. (2008). *Churchill by Himself: The definitive collection of quotations*, London: Ebury.

Lassen, C. (2010). Environmentalist in business class: an analysis of air travel and environmental attitude, *Transport Reviews*, 30(6), 733–751.

Layard, R. (2005). *Happiness: Lessons from a New Science*, London: Allen Lane.

Leach, M., Scoones, I. and Stirling, A. (2010). *Dynamic Sustainabilities: Technology, environment, social justice,* London: Earthscan.

Lecocq, F. (2005). *State and Trends of the Carbon Market 2004*, World Bank Working paper No. 44, Washington, DC: World Bank Publications.

Lee, D.S., Pitari, G., Grewe, V., Gierens, K., Penner, J.E. and Sausen, R. (2010). Transport impacts on atmosphere and climate: Aviation, *Atmospheric Environment*, 44(37), 4678–4734.

Levin, M. and Greenwood, D.J. (2008). The future of universities: action research and the transformation of higher education. In P. Reason and H. Bradbury (eds), *The SAGE handbook of action research: Participative inquiry and practice*, London: SAGE, 211–226.

Lewis, J.I. and Wiser, R.H. (2007). Fostering a renewable energy technology industry: an international comparison of wind industry policy support mechanisms, *Energy Policy*, 35(3), 1844–1857.

Lewis, M. and Conaty, P. (2012). *The Resilience Imperative*, Gabriola Island, Canada: New Society.

Lockwood, M. (2015). The political dynamics of green transformations. In I. Scoones, M. Leach and P. Newell (eds), *The Politics of Green Transformations*, Abingdon: Routledge, 86–101.

Malthus, T.R. (1826). *An Essay on the Principle of Population, or a View of its Past and Present Effects on Human Happiness; with an Inquiry into our Prospects respecting the Future Removal or Mitigation of the Evils which it Occasions*, London: John Murray.

Mander J. (2001). Technologies of globalization. In Edward Goldsmith and Jerry Mander (eds), *The Case Against the Global Economy: And for a turn Towards Localization*, London: Earthscan, 45–57.

Markard, J., Raven, R. and Truffer, B. (2012). Sustainability transitions: an emerging field of research and its prospects, *Research Policy*, Special Section on Sustainability Transitions, 41(6), 955–967.

Martenson, C. (2011). *The Crash Course: The Unsustainable Future of our Economy, Energy, and Environment*, Hoboken, NJ: Wiley.

Martin, R. (2012). Regional economic resilience, hysteresis and recessionary shocks, *Journal of Economic Geography*, 12(1), 1–32.

Martin, R. and Sunley, P. (2015). On the notion of regional economic resilience: conceptualization and explanation, *Economic Geography*, 15, 1–42.

McDonough, W. and Braungart, M. (2002). *Cradle to Cradle: Remaking the way we make things*, New York: North Point Press.

McDonough, W. and Braungart, M. (2013). *The Upcycle: Beyond sustainability – designing for abundance*, New York: Melcher Media.

McManners, P.J. (2008). *Adapt and Thrive: The Sustainable Revolution*, Reading: Susta.

McManners, P.J. (2009). *Victim of Success: Civilization at Risk*, Reading: Susta.

McManners, P.J. (2010). *Green Outcomes in the Real World: Global forces, local circumstances and sustainable solutions*, Farnham: Gower.

McManners, P.J. (2012). *Fly and Be Damned: What now for aviation and climate change?* London: Zed Books.

McManners, P.J. (2014). Reframing economic policy towards sustainability, *Inernational Journal of Green Economics*, 8(3/4), 288–305.

McManners, P.J. (2015). Sustainability in aviation, abstract of presentation at the 5th World Sustainability Forum, *Program and Abstract Book*, Basel: World Sustainability Forum.

McManners, P.J. (2016a). The action research case study approach: A methodology for complex challenges such as sustainability in aviation, *Action Research*, 14(2), 201–216.

McManners, P.J. (2016b). Developing policy integrating sustainability: A case study into aviation, *Environmental Science & Policy*, 57, 86–2.

McNiff, J. and Whitehead, J. (2000). *Action Research in Organisations*, London: Routledge.

Meadows, D.H., Meadows, D.L. and Randers, J. (1972). *The Limits to Growth*, New York: Universe Books.

Meadows, D.H., Randers, J. and Meadows, D. (2004). *Limits to Growth: The 30-Year Update*, White River Junction, VT: Chelsea Green Publishing Company.

Mennes, L.B.M. (1973). *Planning Economic Integration among developing countries*, Rotterdam: Rotterdam University Press.

Meyer, A. (2000). *Contraction & Convergence: The global solution to climate change*, Cambridge: Green Books.

Milanovic, B. (2003). The two faces of globalization: against globalization as we know it, *World Development*, 31(4), 667–683.

Mill, J.S. ([1848] 1909). Of the Stationary State. In *Principles of Political Economy with Some of their Applications to Social Philosophy,* Chap. VI, Book IV, 7th edition, London: Longmans.

Minsky, H.P. (1992). *The Financial Instability Hypothesis*, The Jerome Levy Economics Institute Working Paper (74).

Neumayer, E. (2003). *Weak Versus Strong Sustainability: Exploring the Limits of Two Opposing Paradigms,* Northampton: Edward Elgar.

Newell, P. (2002). A world environment organization: the wrong solution to the wrong problem, *World Economy*, 25(5), 659–671.

Nijkamp, P. (1999). Sustainable transport: new research and policy challenge for the next millennium, *European Review*, 7, 551–563, [DOI: 10.1017/S1062798700004476].

Norgaard, R. (1988). Sustainable development: a coevolutionary view, *Futures*, 606–620.

Obstfeld, M. and Rogoff, K. (2009). Global imbalances and the financial crisis: products of common causes. Paper prepared for the Federal Reserve Bank of San Francisco Asia Economic Policy Conference, Santa Barbara, CA, October 18–20, 2009, [available at: www.parisschoolofeconomics.eu/IMG/pdf/BdF-PSE-IMF_paper_OBSTFELD-ROGOFF.pdf; accessed 30 March 2016].

O'Connor, W.E. (2001). *An Introduction to Airline Economics*, 6th edition, Westport: Praeger.

OECD (2011). *Towards Green Growth*, OECD Green Growth Studies, Paris: OECD Publishing, [DOI: http://dx.doi.org/10.1787/9789264111318-en].

Ormerod, R.J. (1996). Combining management consultancy and research, *Omega, International Journal of Management Science*, 24(1), 1–2.

Owen, B., Lee, D.S. and Ling, L. (2010). Flying into the Future: Aviation: Emissions scenarios to 2050, *Environmental Science & Technology*, 44(7), 2255–2260.

Pearce, D.W. and Atkinson, G.D. (1993). Capital theory and the measurement of sustainable development: an indicator of "weak" sustainability, *Ecological Economics*, 8(2), 103–108.

Pearce, D. and Barbier, E.B. (2000). *Blueprint for a Sustainable Economy*, London: Earthscan.

Peet, R. (2003). *Unholy Trinity: The IMF, World Bank and WTO*, London: Zed Books.

Pelling, M. (2011). *Adaptation to Climate Change: From Resilience to Transformation*, Abingdon: Routledge.

Perovic, J. (2013). The economic benefits of aviation and performance in the travel & tourism competitiveness index. In *The Travel & Tourism Competitiveness Report 2013*, Geneva: World Economic Forum, 57–61.

Peters, S. (2004). Coercive western energy security strategies: 'resource wars' as a new threat to global security, *Geopolitics*, 9(1), 187–212.

Pezzoli, K. (1997). Sustainable development: A transdisciplinary overview of the literature, *Journal of Environmental Planning and Management*, 40(5), 549–574.

Polanyi, K. (2001). *The Great Transformation: The political and economic origins of our time*, Boston: Beacon Press.

Polasky, S. (2012). Economics: conservation in the red, *Nature*, 492, 193–194.

Pollitt, C. (2003). Joined-up government: a survey, *Political Studies Review*, 1(1), 34–39.

Pooley, E. (2010). *The Climate War: True believers, power brokers, and the fight to save the Earth*, New York: Hyperion.

Poteete, A.R., Janssen, M.A. and Ostrom, E. (2010). *Working Together: Collective action, the commons, and multiple methods in practice*, Princetown, NJ: Princeton University Press.

Preston, H., Lee, D.S. and Hooper, P.D. (2012). The inclusion of the aviation sector within the European Union's Emissions Trading Scheme: What are the prospects for a more sustainable aviation industry? *Environmental Development*, 2, 48–56.

Pretty, J. (2003). Social capital and the collective management of resources, *Science*, 302(5652), 1912–1914.

Reason, P. and Bradbury, H. (eds) (2000). *Handbook of Action Research: Participative inquiry and practice*, London: SAGE.

Rees, W.E. (2006). Globalization, trade and migration: undermining sustainability, *Ecological Economics*, 59(2), 220–225.

Remig, M.C. (2015). Unraveling the veil of fuzziness: A thick description of sustainability economics, *Ecological Economics*, 109, 194–202.

Retallack, S. (2006). The environmental cost of economic globalization. In M. Della Guista, U.S. Kambhampati and H.W. Wade (eds), *Critical Perspectives on Globalization*, Cheltenham: Edward Elgar, 314–328.

Ricardo, D. (1817). *On the Principles of Political Economy and Taxation*, London: John Murray.

Rittel, H.W. and Webber, M.M. (1973). Dilemmas in a general theory of planning, *Policy Sciences*, 4(2), 155–69.

Ritzer, G. (2010). *Globalization: A basic text*, Oxford: Wiley-Blackwell.

Robertson, R. (1990). Mapping the global condition: globalization as the central concept. In Mike Featherstone (ed.), *Global Culture: Nationalism, Globalization and Modernity*, London: SAGE.

Rockström, J., Steffen, W., Noone, K., Persson, Å., Chapin III, F.S. and Foley, J. (2009). Planetary boundaries: exploring the safe operating space for humanity, *Ecology and Society*, 14(2), 32, [available at: www.ecologyandsociety.org/vol14/iss2/art32/; accessed 30 March 2016].

Rodrik, D. (2006). Goodbye Washington Consensus, hello Washington confusion? A review of the World Bank's economic growth in the 1990s: learning from a decade of reform, *Journal of Economic Literature*, 44(4), 973–987.

Rodrik, D. (2008). A practical approach to formulating growth strategies. In N. Serra and J.E. Stiglitz (eds), *The Washington Consensus Reconsidered: Towards a new global governance*, Oxford: Oxford University Press, 356–366.

Rubin, H.J. and Rubin, I.S. (2012). *Qualitative Interview: The art of hearing data*, 3rd edition, London: SAGE.

Rumbaugh, T. and Blancher, N. (2004). *China: International trade and WTO accession*, IMF Working Paper No. 04/36, [available at: http://ssrn.com/abstract=878859; accessed 30 March 2016].

Sach, J.D. (2015). *The Age of Sustainable Development*, New York: Columbia University Press.

Salvi, C., Bricolo, E., Kounios, J., Bowden, E. and Beeman, M. (2016). Insight solutions are correct more often than analytic solutions, *Thinking & Reasoning*, 1–8.

Schellenberger, M. and Nordhaus, T. (2009). The death of environmentalism: Global warming politics in a post-environmental world, *Geopolitics, History, and International Relations*, (1), 121–163.

Scherer, F.M. (1986). *Innovation and Growth: Schumpeterian perspectives*, Cambridge, MA: MIT Press Books.

Schiermeier, Q. (2012). The Kyoto Protocol: hot air, *Nature*, 491, 656–658.

Schmitz, H. (2015). Green Transformation: Is there a fast track? In I. Scoones, M. Leach and P. Newell (eds), *The Politics of Green Transformations*, Abingdon: Earthscan, 170–184.

Schneider, M., Hendrichs, H. and Hoffmann, V.H. (2010). Navigating the global carbon market: an analysis of the CDM's value chain and prevalent business models, *Energy Policy*, 38, 277–287.

Schwartz, L.A. and Busby, J. (2014). The 787 Dreamliner: will it be a dream or nightmare for Boeing Co.? *Journal of Case Research in Business and Economics*, 5, 1.

Scoones, I., Leach, M. and Newell, P. (eds) (2015). *The Politics of Green Transformations*, Abingdon: Earthscan.

Scott, J.C. (1998). *Seeing Like a State: How certain schemes to improve the human condition have failed*, New Haven: Yale University Press.

SDC (2007). *Findings from the SD Panel Debate, Aviation – Second Session*, [available at: www.sd-commission.org.uk/data/files/publications/SDPanelAviationReport Session2.pdf; accessed 30 March 2016].

SDC (2008a). Breaking the holding pattern: a new approach to aviation policymaking in the UK, [available at: www.sd-commission.org.uk/data/files/publications/sdc_aviation_exec_summ1.pdf; accessed 30 March 2016].

SDC (2008b). Summary report of facilitated events and aviation site visits, Annex 3 to Breaking the holding pattern, [available at: www.sd-commission.org.uk/data/files/publications/Breaking_the_holding_pattern_annex3.pdf; accessed 30 March 2016].

SDC (2008c). Stakeholder assessment of aviation in the UK: an evaluation by Icarus Collective, April 2008, [available at: www.sd-commission.org.uk/data/files/publications/aviation_stakeholder_assessment.pdf; accessed 30 March 2016].

Sekeris, P.G. (2014). The tragedy of the commons in a violent world, *The RAND Journal of Economics*, 45, 521–532.

Serra, N., Spiegel, S. and Stiglitz, J.E. (2008). Introduction: from the Washington consensus towards a new global governance. In N. Serra and J.E. Stiglitz (eds), *The Washington Consensus Reconsidered: Towards a New Global Governance,* Oxford: Oxford University Press, 1ff.

Shiva, V. (2006). War against nature and the people of the south. In M. Della Guista, U.S. Kambhampati and H.W. Wade (eds), *Critical Perspectives on Globalization*, Cheltenham: Edward Elgar, 279–313.

Skole, D.L. (2004). Geography as a great intellectual melting pot and the preeminent interdisciplinary environmental discipline, *Annals of the Association of American Geographers*, 94(4), 739–743.

Smith, A. (1759). *The Theory of the Moral Sentiments*, London: Millar.

Smith, A. (1776). *An Inquiry into the Nature and Causes of the Wealth of Nations*, London: Strahan and Cadell.

Söderbaum, P. (2008). *Understanding Sustainability Economics: Towards Pluralism in Economics*, London: Earthscan.

Sparke, M. (2006). Political geography: political geographies of globalization (2) – governance, *Progress in Human Geography*, 30(3), 357.

Sperling, G. (2007). Rising-tide economics, *Democracy* (2007), 1–4.

SSEE (2010). *Future of Mobility Roadmap*, 2nd edition, Oxford: Smith School of Enterprise and the Environment (SSEE).

Steinbruner, J.D., Stern P.C. and Husbands J.L. (2012). *Climate and Social Stress: Implications for Security Analysis*, Washington, DC: National Academies Press.

Stern, N. (2007). *The Economics of Climate Change: The Stern Review*, Cambridge: Cambridge University Press.

Stern, N.H. (2015). *Why are we Waiting? The logic, urgency and promise of tackling climate change*, Cambridge, MA: MIT Press.

Stettler, M.E.J., Eastham, S. and Barrett, S.R.H. (2011). Air quality and public health impacts of UK airports. Part I: Emissions, *Atmospheric Environment*, 45(31), 5415–5424.

Steurer, R. and Berger, G. (2011). The EU's double-track pursuit of sustainable development in the 2000s: how Lisbon and sustainable development strategies ran past each other, *International Journal of Sustainable Development & World Ecology*, 18(2), 99–108.

Stiglitz, J.E. (2002). *Globalization and its Discontents*, London: Allen Lane.

Stiglitz, J.E. (2006). *Making Globalization Work*, London: Allen Lane.

Stiglitz, J.E. (2008). The Future of Global Governance. In N. Serra and J.E. Stiglitz (eds), *The Washington Consensus Reconsidered: Towards a new global governance*, Oxford: Oxford University Press.

Summers, D. (2008). No return to boom and bust: what Brown said when he was chancellor, *Guardian*, [available at: www.theguardian.com/politics/2008/sep/11/gordonbrown.economy; accessed 30 March 2016].

Sunley, P. (2011). The consequences of economic globalization. In A. Leyshon, R. Lee, L. McDowell and P. Sunley (eds), *The SAGE Handbook of Economic Geography*, London: SAGE, 102–118.

Sustainable Aviation (2012). *Sustainable Aviation CO₂ Road Map 2012*, London: Sustainable Aviation.

Sustainable Aviation (2014). *Sustainable Fuels UK Road-Map*, London: Sustainable Aviation.

Söderbaum, P. (2008). *Understanding Sustainability Economics. Towards pluralism in economics*, London: Earthscan.

Tainter, J. (1988). *The Collapse of Complex Societies*, Cambridge: Cambridge University Press.

Tan, X. and Rose, B. (2007). A geospatial approach to sustainability study, *International Journal of Sustainable Development*, 10(3), 214–232.

Therborn, G. (2000). Globalizations: dimensions, historical waves, regional effects, normative governance, *International Sociology*, 15(2), 151–179.

Truffer, B., Murphy, J.T. and Raven, R. (2015). The geography of sustainability transitions contours of an emerging theme, *Environmental Innovation and Societal Transitions*, 17, 63–72.

Trulove, J.G. (2006). *New Sustainable Homes: Designs for healthy living*, New York: Harper Collins.

Turner, A. (2009). The Turner Review: a regulatory response to the global banking crisis, London: Financial Services Authority, [available at: www.fsa.gov.uk/pubs/other/turner_review.pdf; accessed 30 March 2016].

UNCTAD (2012). *Trade and Development Report, 1981–2011: Three decades of thinking development*, Geneva: United Nations.

UNEP (2012). *Global Environmental Outlook: 5 Environment for the future we want*, Nairobi: United Nations Environment Programme.

UNEP (2015). *UNEP 2014 Annual Report*, [available at: www.unep.org/annualreport/2014/en/index.html; accessed 30 March 2016].

UNFCCC (1995). *Report of the Conference of the Parties on Its First Session, Held At Berlin from 28 March to 7 April 1995*, document FCCC/CP/1995/7/Add.1, 6 June 1995.

UNFCCC (2009). *Report of the Subsidiary Body for Scientific and Technological Advice on its Twenty-Ninth Session, Held in Poznan from 1 to 10 December 2008*, document FCCC/SBSTA/2008/13, 17 February 2009.

UNFCCC (2013). *Report of the Subsidiary Body for Scientific and Technological Advice on its Thirty-Ninth Session, Held in Warsaw from 11 to 17 November 2013*, document FCCC/SBSTA/2013/5, 18 December 2013.

UNFCCC (2015). Adoption of the Paris Agreement, UNFCCC COP 21 Paris 30 Nov–11 Dec 2015, [available at: http://unfccc.int/resource/docs/2015/cop21/eng/l09.pdf; accessed 30 March 2016].

United Nations Secretary-General's High-Level Panel on Global Sustainability, (2012), *Resilient People, Resilient Planet: A future worth choosing, Overview*, New York: United Nations.

van den Bergh, J.C.J.M. and Verbruggen, H. (1999). Spatial sustainability, trade and indicators: an evaluation of the 'ecological footprint', *Ecological Economics*, 29, 61–72.

Vasigh, B., Fleming, K. and Tacker, T. (2008). *Introduction to Air Transport Economics*, Farnham: Ashgate.

Veseth, M. (2005). *Globaloney: Unravelling the myths of globalization*, Lanham, MD: Rowman and Littlefield.

Victor, P. (2010). Questioning economic growth, *Nature*, 468, 370–371.

Walker, S. and Cook, M. (2009). The contested concept of sustainable aviation, *Sustainable Development*, 17(6), 378–390.

Watson, C. (2014). *Beyond Flying: Rethinking air travel in a globally connected world*, Cambridge: Green Books.

WCED (1987). *Our Common Future*, Oxford: Oxford University Press.

Weaver, P.M. and Jordan, A. (2008). What roles are there for sustainability assessment in the policy process? *International Journal of Innovation and Sustainable Development*, 3(1/2), 9–32.

WEF (2013). *Global Risks 2013 Eighth Edition: An initiative of the Risk Response Network*, Geneva: World Economic Forum.

Wiebe, K.S., Bruckner, M., Giljum, S. and Lutz, C. (2012). Calculating energy-related CO_2 emissions embodied in international trade using a global input–output model, *Economic Systems Research*, 24(2), 113–139.

Williamson, J. (2008). A short history of the Washington consensus. In N. Serra and J.E. Stiglitz (eds), *The Washington Consensus Reconsidered: Towards a new global governance*, Oxford: Oxford University Press, 14–30.

Wolf, M. (2004). *Why Globalization Works*, New Haven, CT: Yale University Press.

WWF (2012). Global Footprint Network Living Planet Report 2012: Biodiversity, biocapacity and better choices, [available at: www.footprintnetwork.org/images/uploads/LPR_2012.pdf; accessed 29 March 2016].

Yin, R. (2014). *Case Study Research: Design and methods,* 5th edition, London: SAGE.

Zalasiewicz, J., Williams, M., Steffen, W. and Crutzen, P. (2010). The New World of the Anthropocene, *Environmental Science & Technology*, 44(7), 2228–2231.

Index

Taylor & Francis eBooks

Helping you to choose the right eBooks for your Library

Add Routledge titles to your library's digital collection today. Taylor and Francis ebooks contains over 50,000 titles in the Humanities, Social Sciences, Behavioural Sciences, Built Environment and Law.

Choose from a range of subject packages or create your own!

Benefits for you

» Free MARC records
» COUNTER-compliant usage statistics
» Flexible purchase and pricing options
» All titles DRM-free.

REQUEST YOUR **FREE** INSTITUTIONAL TRIAL TODAY

Free Trials Available
We offer free trials to qualifying academic, corporate and government customers.

Benefits for your user

» Off-site, anytime access via Athens or referring URL
» Print or copy pages or chapters
» Full content search
» Bookmark, highlight and annotate text
» Access to thousands of pages of quality research at the click of a button.

eCollections – Choose from over 30 subject eCollections, including:

Archaeology	Language Learning
Architecture	Law
Asian Studies	Literature
Business & Management	Media & Communication
Classical Studies	Middle East Studies
Construction	Music
Creative & Media Arts	Philosophy
Criminology & Criminal Justice	Planning
Economics	Politics
Education	Psychology & Mental Health
Energy	Religion
Engineering	Security
English Language & Linguistics	Social Work
Environment & Sustainability	Sociology
Geography	Sport
Health Studies	Theatre & Performance
History	Tourism, Hospitality & Events

For more information, pricing enquiries or to order a free trial, please contact your local sales team:
www.tandfebooks.com/page/sales

Routledge
Taylor & Francis Group

The home of
Routledge books

www.tandfebooks.com

For Product Safety Concerns and Information please contact our EU
representative GPSR@taylorandfrancis.com
Taylor & Francis Verlag GmbH, Kaufingerstraße 24, 80331 München, Germany

www.ingramcontent.com/pod-product-compliance
Ingram Content Group UK Ltd.
Pitfield, Milton Keynes, MK11 3LW, UK
UKHW020948180425
457613UK00019B/589